GETTING STARTED IN

STOCK

INVESTING & TRADING

ILLUSTRATED EDITION

GETTING STARTED IN
STOCK
INVESTING & TRADING

ILLUSTRATED EDITION

MICHAEL C. THOMSETT

WILEY

Cover design and illustration: Kestrel.

Published by John Wiley & Sons Singapore Pte. Ltd.
1 Fusionopolis Walk, #07-01, Solaris South Tower, Singapore 138628

Other Wiley Editorial Offices
John Wiley & Sons, 111 River Street, Hoboken, NJ 07030, USA
John Wiley & Sons, The Atrium, Southern Gate, Chichester, West Sussex, PO19 8SQ, United Kingdom
John Wiley& Sons (Canada) Ltd., 5353 Dundas Street West, Suite 400, Toronto, Ontario, M9B 6HB, Canada
John Wiley& Sons Australia Ltd., 42 McDougall Street, Milton, Queensland 4064, Australia
Wiley-VCH, Boschstrasse 12, D-69469 Weinheim, Germany

ISBN 978-1-118-39925-5 (Paperback)
ISBN 978-1-118-39929-3 (ePDF)
ISBN 978-1-118-39928-6 (Mobi)
ISBN 978-1-118-39927-9 (ePub)

Typeset in 11pt. Adobe Garamond Pro.
Printed in the United States of America.

10 9 8 7 6 5 4 3 2 1

CONTENTS

ACKNOWLEDGMENTS

Thanks to those many readers who wrote to offer their suggestions and insights to previous editions of this book, including constructive criticism and clarifying questions. Their letters have helped to improve the ever-changing sets of explanations and examples, definitions, and other materials used in this book.

A very special thanks goes to Debra Englander, my editor for many years at John Wiley & Sons, whose encouragement through many editions of this and other books has been greatly appreciated.

Also, my thanks to Nick Wallwork and Gemma Rosey, whose editorial guidance on this edition was so valuable and professional.

ELEMENT KEY

Definitions
This symbol is found in boxed notations providing specific definitions of options terms. These are placed within the book to accompany and augment discussions relevant to each definition

Key Points
These highlighted sections emphasize key points or add observations, rules of thumb, resources, and added points that options traders can use.

Valuable Resources
These sections provide links to web sites where you will find added value for particular options discussions, to further help in expanding your options knowledge base.

Examples
Numerous examples illustrate points raised in context and provide a view of how the issues might apply using actual options trades. This is intended to demonstrate practical application of the principles being presented.

INTRODUCTION

The stock market has become known as a volatile place to invest. Many risks and opportunities are available to investors and traders alike. Any novice stock market investor needs to develop a complete understanding of the risks they face when money is placed in the market.

This does not mean you should avoid investing; it does point out how important it is to become educated about risk in the stock market. There are no fast or easy ways to gain knowledge or a trading edge. Paid services, the Internet, and financial planners all offer expert services, but in the final analysis it all comes down to each individual learning for themselves what works and what does not.

Are you an investor or a trader? This book makes a distinction between investing and trading. An investor is an individual interested in identifying and buying shares of stock for long term price appreciation, also called growth; and earning superior returns from dividends while protecting their capital. Part 1 of this book includes chapters about how to develop an investing program to build your portfolio based on the principles of fundamental analysis.

A trader is more interested in moving in and out of investment positions in the short term, making a higher volume of smaller profits. Traders rely on reading charts, spotting short-term trends, and taking advantage of the market's tendency to overreact to current news (meaning that the prices of stocks tend to move too far in one direction, and then correct by reversing). This price swing is easy to spot in hindsight, but more difficult to anticipate ahead of time. Successful traders work on their skills in identifying the signs based on price charts. Part 2 is focused on trading skills and techniques, and is based on the principles of technical analysis.

The purpose in compiling this book is to present you with a range of ideas, strategies, and market realities, all aimed at helping you to identify your appropriate risk tolerance level, and then determine which investing and trading ideas are going to work best for you. Everyone is different, so no quick fix or formula is going to work for everyone. In fact, trying to duplicate someone else's investing or trading system is not a wise idea because your unique profile (including income, assets, experience, and perceptions of markets and risks) demand that your approach makes sense.

Today, many people are shy about the market. The volatility of recent years is a definite problem for anyone who puts capital at risk, but does that mean that staying out of the market makes sense? It does not. The alternatives are bleak. Savings rates are lower than ever before and do not outpace inflation. This means that even the modest inflation of recent years erodes the purchasing power of money left in savings. The only sensible alternative is to develop a program of investing and trading that minimizes risk while offering superior returns. Avoiding the market is just as great a problem as taking too many risks within the market; so the best approach is to develop a portfolio defensively.

A "defensively" built portfolio is one that is developed with complete knowledge about risk and opportunity, which you build and manage based on thorough research, acquired knowledge, and resistance of market forces. This book is designed with this necessity in mind. In the future, markets will go through cycles of relatively low volatility, followed by highly erratic months or even years. Investors and traders can earn profits in all kinds of markets, assuming that they have built a defensive portfolio and avoided taking risks they cannot afford. This makes it essential not only to understand risks, but also to define where you fit in the risk spectrum. Most people are going to be somewhere in the middle between extreme conservatism and extreme speculation, but that is a broad range. For this reason, both of the first two sections of the book begin with chapters examining and explaining a range of different risks.

The purpose in this endeavor is not to provide easy answers, but to help you to begin your journey into acquiring knowledge about a complex and changing stock market. Knowledge reduces risk and increases profit. This is the basic premise that has dominated the preparation of this book.

Since publishing the first edition, the markets have become even more volatile than in the past. This is in some respects a disturbing trend because it means that risks are high for everyone. However, in another sense volatile markets present many opportunities that are not to be found in calmer, less volatile investing environments.

Several new features have been added to this edition. This illustrated edition is designed to appeal visually as well as to greatly improve on the connection between graphics and text.

A new Chapter 1 describes the nature of stock investing by examining common myths and beliefs. A new Chapter 6 discusses dividend strategies. Many investors ignore the importance of dividends; but this form of income may represent a very important segment of overall returns.

In Part 2, Chapter 8 has been added to set up the following chapters with an examination of the nature of stock trading. In Chapter 13, you find a summary of signals and confirmation of price movement.

These new chapters, together with updated chapters from the first edition, provide novices with an overview of the market; and provide more experienced investors and traders with an important overview of how the market works, keeping risk in mind, and setting up policies and goals to enhance your success in the ever-changing and volatile stock market.

GETTING STARTED IN

STOCK

INVESTING & TRADING

ILLUSTRATED EDITION

PART 1 **INVESTING**

1 THE NATURE OF STOCK INVESTING

The stock market has a strong allure. This is because it appeals both to the imagination and the profit motive of anyone trying to save money, earn profit, or save for the future.

The imagination aspect of the market allows you to see how it is possible to turn a pool of capital into a much larger pool, to beat the odds and the averages, and to set yourself up with security for the future. The truth is that this is entirely possible, but much more difficult to accomplish. The relationship between risk and opportunity is inescapable; so making that quick fortune is not as easy as anyone wishes.

Key Point
Opportunity and risk are directly related as two sides of the same coin. As one increases or decreases, so does the other. This relationship between opportunity and risk is an essential concept in successful investing.

Profit motive is equally as compelling. Everyone would like to be able to outperform the safe and secure guaranteed savings account, which yields so little that it loses purchasing power over time. If inflation is higher than the rate you are paid, leaving money in an insured account eats away at your capital. Added to this is the effect of income taxes. Taken together, inflation and taxes make it virtually impossible to accumulate value over time and in real terms.

These are the reasons for the allure of the stock market.

simple interest

Interest calculated at its annual rate and without compounding; for example, dividend yield represents the simple interest paid on stock each year.

compound interest

Interest calculated at a periodic rate based on the stated annual rate. For example, a 4 percent interest rate compounded quarterly represents compound annual interest of 4.06 percent (1.01 x 1.01 x 1.01 x 1.01) = 1.0406, or 4.06 percent.

FAVORABLE CONDITIONS FOR OWNING STOCKS

The market contains many aspects favoring ownership of stocks, and is a matter of balancing risk against reward. These aspects include:

1. Dividend income. Many stocks pay dividends, meaning a regular quarterly source of income. Dividends might look quite small, but they add up. If you reinvest dividends to purchase additional partial shares, you turn *simple interest* into *compound interest*. That means your money grows faster. In addition, many companies pay a very attractive interest rate. For example, over 650 listed stocks yield between 4 and 6 percent per year.[1]

2. Favorable tax treatment. Both dividends and *capital gains* may be taxed at lower rates than other income. For capital gains, the tax rate is based on the holding period of stock; so the tax code provides an incentive for people to invest in stocks.

3. Flexibility. Investing in stocks is a flexible matter. The market is set up to accommodate investment in a number of variations. These include owning stock directly, ownership through mutual funds or exchange-traded funds, and even more advanced methods such as trading of options on listed stocks. The market is set up to respond to what investors and traders want.

[1] *Source:* Charles Schwab & Co., stock research function.

4. Affordability. In the modern market, the cost of trading stocks is very low. Online discount brokerage services are available for anyone willing to make decisions without a stockbroker's advice, with trades costing less than $10. In the past, trading was relatively quite expensive.

5. Access. The Internet has brought down the cost and expanded the markets to more people than ever before. This is a great benefit, but the evolution of access has also created many problems. For example, it is possible to trade quite actively, meaning more people today move in and out of stocks in very short time periods. Some market observers think this is detrimental to the markets, while others believe it is simply the way that people prefer to use the access itself. The speed of the Internet makes trade execution virtually instantaneous in most cases, so traders can place orders and then see the executed final price seconds later.

capital gains

Profits on investments such as stocks, taxed at a lower rate than other income if the asset is owned for one year or more.

Key Point
The five aspects making stock investing attractive are dividend income, favorable tax treatment, flexibility, affordability, and access.

The greater convenience, higher access, and lower costs of today's stock market means that investment goals also change with time. A half century ago, traders tended to hold stocks for many years and the standard was to buy stocks and wait for profits to accumulate over those many years. Today, average holding periods are measured in weeks or even days rather than in years; this is due to the access and affordability of trading. Many people prefer shorter holding periods over longer ones, and attempt to trade the fluctuations in price. Market volatility—another name for risk—is seen by many as an attractive opportunity rather than as a problem.

RELATIONSHIPS BETWEEN PRICE AND FUNDAMENTAL VALUE

A debate goes on continuously among market experts as well as between investors and traders. What is best, fundamental or technical analysis? A fundamental investor relies on the financial trends of the company to identify value. A technical analyst tracks price movement, seeking short-term trends, momentum changes, and reversal signals. Both have valid arguments but come from a different point of view.

The fact is, both fundamental and technical approaches are valid and even represent different aspects of the same broader analysis. The study of any 10-year trend of a company and its stock demonstrate that when the fundamentals are strong, the stock's price rises; and equally important, when the fundamentals grow weaker, the price level also falls.

Key Point

Both fundamental and technical analysis offer worthwhile attributes that investors can use to improve their stock selection and portfolio management skills.

To make this point, consider two different companies on the extremes of change over 10 years. Looking at two indicators, one technical and the other fundamental, demonstrates the direct relationship between the two. First is the price range, a technical indicator. In a successful and well-managed company, you expect to see the range from high to low each year increase over a decade. If this is the case, the company probably represents a worthwhile investment. If the price level declines, that is a very negative indicator. As a long-term technical signal, it is revealing. Why would anyone want to buy stock in a company whose price range falls each year?

The second indicator is one of the most reliable tests of fundamental strength or weakness. The debt ratio measures the percentage of long-term borrowing to total capitalization. (The total consists of long-term borrowing and shareholders' equity.) This topic is covered in more detail in later chapters. For now, it is only necessary to understand that the ratio, expressed as a single number, represents the percentage of debt to the total (of debt and equity). In a well-run company you expect to see the debt ratio remain steady over time or even to decline. In a poorly run company or one on the way to bankruptcy, the debt ratio climbs each year.

If the debt ratio is over 100 percent, it means the company is holding long-term debt more than the entire equity. In other words, the equity value is zero because debt is out of control.

Key Point

Debt is only part of the capitalization picture; so if the debt ratio is over 100 percent, it means the equity value of the company is lower than zero. This is why analysis of long-term debt is critical in stock selection.

The comparison is made here between Eastman Kodak (EK) and McDonald's (MCD). Both of these are American icons, although Kodak's best days appear to be in the past. Early in 2012, the company announced its intention to file for bankruptcy protection. Meanwhile, McDonald's has been one of the best-performing stocks over the past few years, and has reported strong growth in profits as well.

Eastman Kodak has been around for over 100 years. Its founder, George Eastman, based his company on the slogan, "You press the button, we do the rest." Its primary product was always film of the highest quality. Its use as well as development was simplified over many decades. In 1883, he pioneered film in rolls and the first preloaded camera. Once customers took pictures, the entire camera was shipped to Kodak in Rochester, New York, where the film was developed, prints were made, and new film put into the camera and sent back.

For its day, the ease and convenience of a preloaded camera was amazing. Kodak continued to make great advances in film throughout the twentieth century. However, in the 1990s the company failed to realize that the days of film were coming to an end. With the advance of digital cameras and film-free photo generation, fewer new customers relied on old-style loaded film and development. Competitors had several years on Kodak by the time it got into the business. As a consequence, Kodak's price range over the decade between 2001 and 2010 fell from as high as $50 down to under $5. In January 2012, the stock price was under $1. The illustration of this 10-year decline in price is shown in Figure 1.1.

Figure 1.1 Eastman Kodak, 10-Year Price History
Source: S&P Stock Reports.

In comparison, Kodak's debt ratio during the same 10 years demonstrated what happens when a company loses its market and declines in basic financial strength. With a debt ratio at the end of fiscal 2001 of 37 (meaning debt was 37 percent of capitalization and shareholders' equity was 63 percent), the company's fortunes fell quickly. By the end of fiscal 2010, the debt ratio had risen to 160 (meaning that debt was 160 percent of total capitalization, and equity was −60 percent). This history of the company's debt ratio is summarized in Figure 1.2.

Notice how the sharp decline in the price range moves opposite the even sharper growth in the debt ratio. Together, these trends spell the path to bankruptcy previously seen by icons like General Motors, Lehman Brothers, Delta Airlines, and Pacific Gas and Electric, to name only a few.

Key Point

A stark reality about debt: When the ratio rises every year and approaches 100 percent of capitalization, it is a warning sign that the company is heading for its demise.

Figure 1.2 Eastman Kodak, 10-Year Debt Ratio History
Source: S&P Stock Reports.

McDonald's is a similar story of success, a company founded by an entrepreneur, with years of growth and expansion. The difference, though, is that McDonald's has been one of the best-performing stocks in recent years. To measure this, check the same two trends, the price range over 10 years (a technical indicator) and the debt ratio (a fundamental indicator).

McDonald's was founded in 1937 by the original McDonald, Patrick; the restaurant was called the Airdrome and it was in Monrovia, California. The 10-cent hamburger was a big hit. In 1940, his two sons moved the restaurant to San Bernardino, California, and renamed it McDonald's. In 1953, they began franchising the idea. Ray Kroc, a salesman who marketed the Multimixer milkshake machine, suggested the McDonald brothers expand their franchises nationally. They were not willing to take that risk so Kroc volunteered to do it for them.

Today, Kroc is recognized as the driving force behind expansion of the chain through the United States and overseas. By 1992, two-thirds of all sales were derived from U.S. locations, but five years later, sales were about 50–50 between U.S. and overseas restaurants. By 1997, there were 12,500 restaurants worldwide. By 2011, the company had created over 33,000 franchisers with total revenues of nearly $77 billion. The corporate model for the company is considered one of the best and most successful.

McDonald's has succeeded not only because it aggressively expanded its business, but also because the organization is professionally operated. A study of the 10-year price range makes this point, as shown in Figure 1.3.

From a modest low of $25 per share in 2001, the fiscal 2010 values ranged between $61 and $81. The strong growth in price from 2008 to 2010 occurred during a period when many companies were in trouble, and during poor economic times. McDonald's has been one of the strongest performers on the New York Stock Exchange.

The technical record of growing prices is matched by an equally strong fundamental indicator found in the company's debt ratio. This has ranged over 10 years from a low of 31 to a high of 46. The debt ratio at the end of 2010 is about the same as it was a decade earlier. This consistency is highly desirable. It shows that while the company was expanding rapidly, it did not increase its long-term debt. Figure 1.4 shows the decade of McDonald's debt ratio.

These indicators make an important point about how you can study a company to decide whether or not to own its stock. The case of Eastman Kodak demonstrates that even a company that has been around for over a century can become obsolete and decline in comparison to its competitors. McDonald's has shown with its history that well-managed companies can expand in terms of price in the market as well as geographic influence, and without taking on greater debt.

Figure 1.3 McDonald's, 10-Year Price History
Source: S&P Stock Reports.

Figure 1.4 McDonald's, 10-Year Debt Ratio History
Source: S&P Stock Reports.

Key Point
An established company with decades of history is
reassuring as a potential investment—unless the numbers
reveal that a decline is underway.

These comparisons are stark in the differences they reveal. Although
in different industries, this is a crucial point about stock investing: It
does not matter as much which sector a company is in or even what its
products and services are. What matters the most is how well the company is managed. This means management has to be able to change its
business model and even its products, and capitalize on what does work.
Kodak was one of the greatest companies in history, but when its primary
product, film, became obsolete for the most part, the company did not
recognize that they needed to evolve. Today, Kodak is pursuing the digital
camera market, but their many competitors are far ahead of them.

An equally important lesson is learned from McDonald's. Kroc was
originally interested in seeing the company expand because he wanted to
sell more milkshake machines. He quickly realized, though, that his own
fortunes resided in creating his own franchises. He saw that the McDonald's idea was a goldmine: cheap, fast, quality food. The American travel-
ers knew what to expect at each location along the road. Expanding to
the international market was a crucial step that expanded the company's
profits.

So while Kodak became mired in an out of style product of the past,
McDonald's recognized the value of maintaining simplicity of product,
and offering it over a wider market.

As an investor, you will be most likely to succeed when you study
companies in a similar manner. There is much more to fundamental and
technical analysis than price range and debt ratio, of course; and these
examples are the extremes. But they make an important point about the

nature of investing, and this brings up the important basic guidelines for picking companies and developing your investment philosophy:

1. **Know the business the company is in.** Also study where that company stands in relation to its competitors and where it is located.
2. **Be aware of growth.** Is the company expanding or shrinking? Is the product growing in demand or becoming obsolete?
3. **Track several indicators**, both fundamental and technical, in order to judge a company's strength or weakness.
4. **Always track the trend.** If you can study 10 years of indicators, you have a healthy understanding of how a company's numbers are getting better or worse.

With these guidelines as your starting point in deciding where to invest, you will have a strong start in picking stocks. Too many first-time investors invest in reaction to advice from others, rumors, or other types of impulse. If you know someone who invests, ask them questions based on the four guidelines above: What business is the company in and where does it get its income? Has the company grown over the past decade? What indicators do you follow? What is the 10-year trend?

Key Point
Ask the basic questions about the company. You will be surprised to learn that even those recommending a stock might not know anything about the company, its product, growth record, or trends.

You might be surprised to discover that many people—perhaps even a majority—cannot answer these questions, even though they form the first line of decision-making in a wise investment policy. If you make sure you can answer these questions about any stock you buy, you will be far ahead of "the crowd" of stock market investors.

To begin deciding what kind of stocks you should buy, the first step is to define companies in terms of these four questions. The next step is to understand, define, and evaluate market risks. The next chapter examines the many types of risks you face as an investor.

THE ADVENTURES OF STOCK MAN

WORKING IN A MUNDANE, *DEAD-END* JOB IN A *SECOND-RATE MARKET* IN A STRIP MALL SOMEWHERE SOUTH OF *DOWNTOWN*...

..."*STOCK BOY*" LIVES HIS LIFE OF QUIET DESPAIR.

CHAPTER 2

INVESTMENT RISKS

Investing in stocks is an exciting, action-packed, fast-moving idea that for decades has excited many people—even those with little money to invest—with the possibility of building wealth.

It is possible to make money in stocks, but it is also possible to lose. The whole question of *risk*—exposure to losses due to a variety of causes—determines how slowly or quickly values change and which kinds of stock positions you end up taking. There are many industry sectors in the market, and each has its own risk characteristics. Some are especially sensitive to changes in interest rates, and others exist within a very specific market *cycle* of changes in profits.

Do you know the range of risks you face as an investor? Some people think that the sole risk they face is directly related to profitability. If you make a profit, you beat the risk; if you have a loss, you lose.

While this distinction is at the core of most investment plans, it is not the whole story. Every investor wants to earn a profit on every investment decision made. However, experienced investors also understand that it's a percentage game. You are going to have some losses along the way, and the key to succeeding is creating profits that are higher than the occasional loss, and for which the dollar amount is much greater.

cycle

An economic tendency for sales volume and profits to change predictably due to economic or calendar timing. Among the best-known of market cycles is that experienced in the retail trade, which goes through specific seasons of high and low sales volume based on consumer buying habits.

Key Point

The purpose in setting up a portfolio wisely is not in completely avoiding risk, but in deciding how to manage it.

This chapter examines a number of different risks every investor faces. It is not simply a matter of profits versus losses, but a more complex series of conflicts between supply and demand, timing, influences in and out of the market, and the economic climate. In other words, many things affect your portfolio and add to or take away from your spectrum of risk whenever you have money in the market.

MARKET RISK

Most people understand the most obvious form of risk, known as market risk, or exposure to declining prices. This is only the first of many risks every investor faces and needs to manage.

Managing risk refers to how you structure your investments to maximize profits while minimizing the chance of losses. This requires careful selection of stocks based on sensible criteria, avoiding putting too much capital into any one stock, and continually monitoring the market to spot changing trends. It also requires that when considering any one company as a possible investment, you know what trends to examine and how to determine market risk based on the indicators you pick and track.

Will the value rise or fall? Realistically, you should understand that a stock's market value may either rise or fall. As apparent as this seems, some investors assume that their entry price is the zero point and that prices will rise from that level as soon as a buy trade is entered. This ignores the reality that prices can also fall. So managing market risk comes down to how well you select stocks and, equally important, how well you time the decision to buy. The better you are able to pick stocks appropriate for you and to determine when to buy *shares*, the less exposure you will have to market risk. The price changes are caused by many factors, but as a general rule, the concept of *supply and demand* determines the value of shares.

Market risk is the ultimate expression of supply and demand. After you purchase shares, many changes can occur. If the demand for a company's shares is quite strong, prices will continue to rise; if demand is weak, prices might fall. When the supply and demand for shares are about equal, the price tends to stay within a narrow range. This condi-

shares

Part ownership of a corporation that is listed publicly. Shares are bought and sold over public exchanges. Owners of shares are entitled to receive dividends and common stock owners are allowed to vote on matters of corporate management. Shares of stock rise and fall in value every day based on the ever-changing levels of supply and demand.

tion, known as *consolidation*, is best described as a time of indecision. No one can tell whether buyers or sellers are in command and, as a result, it is impossible to predict whether the next price direction will be upward or downward.

Market risk is easily observed in hindsight. Everyone can see when they should have bought shares and, just as important, when they should have sold. For anyone interested in creating a long-term portfolio of profitable holdings, there are 10 general guidelines for managing market risk:

1. Research a company before buying stock.
2. Look for changes after you buy shares.
3. Be aware of market cycles for the sector.
4. Know a company's position within the sector, remembering that the leader tends to outperform other companies.
5. Develop a list of criteria you consider most essential for narrowing down your choices.
6. Use past trends to predict how the future might look.
7. Give up some short-term opportunities gladly, in exchange for longer-term certainty.
8. Pick a wise plan and don't veer away from it.
9. Establish clear short-term and long-term goals and use these as guides for the decisions you make.
10. Never make a decision just because the majority is making the same decision; be a *contrarian* investor.

These are very preliminary suggestions that are expanded in coming chapters. However, the points above do provide you with an idea of how to pick stocks, which is at the heart of how you manage and reduce market risk.

supply and demand

The economic forces that set prices for publicly traded stocks. When buyers want more shares than are immediately available from sellers, the excess demand drives up prices. When sellers want to sell more shares than buyers want to buy, the excess supply forces prices down. The interactive supply and demand forces are continuous.

consolidation

A period of indecision in the market, during which neither buyers nor sellers are in command. No one can determine whether prices will be driven higher or lower, so there is little or no movement during this time.

contrarian

An investor or trader who makes decisions based on analysis rather than simply following the majority, and who recognizes that the majority is wrong more often than right, so making the opposite decision often is the smart move.

LEVERAGE RISK

Among the many forms of risk, *leverage risk* poses one of the greatest threats to your financial health. This is the risk that arises when investors borrow money to buy stocks.

Most people will agree that it would be foolish to mortgage a home to the hilt to free up money to enter the stock market. The same people would not think it wise to seek a bank loan or line of credit to expand their portfolio. However, many of the same people will use a brokerage firm's margin account without hesitation. This is a form of borrowing. The *margin account* can be used to double up your positions.

Examples

Double or Nothing: If you have $20,000 to invest, you can take up positions as high as $40,000 under the rule that you have to maintain at least one-half of value in cash and securities. The rest can be borrowed in your margin account.

Valuable Resource

To review the rules governing margin trading and margin maintenance, go to
www.sec.gov/investor/pubs/margin.htm.

A margin account is a great convenience, but using it increases your risk. If you expand $20,000 to $40,000 and it earns 25 percent, you make a $10,000 profit. On only $20,000 in the same investment, you would earn only half of that, or $5,000. So the case for using leverage with a margin account is a strong one—until you consider what happens in cases of loss.

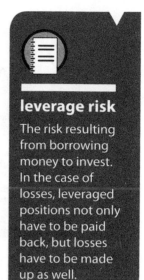

leverage risk

The risk resulting from borrowing money to invest. In the case of losses, leveraged positions not only have to be paid back, but losses have to be made up as well.

Examples

Accelerated Loss: If you start out with $20,000 in cash and borrow another $20,000 on margin, what happens if the $40,000 portfolio loses 25 percent? It falls to $30,000. Two things happen right away. First, your broker will issue a margin call, meaning you are required to meet minimum maintenance requirements, or keep 50 percent in the form of cash and securities.

In the example, the portfolio's overall value has fallen to $30,000 but $20,000 of that was borrowed in the margin account. So your capital value has fallen to only $10,000. The broker will issue a $10,000 *margin call*, meaning you have to bring your $10,000 of capital up to match the amount on margin, $20,000. If you cannot come up with the amount demanded by the margin call, your broker will sell off $10,000 of your holdings to pay down the margin. This results in a portfolio worth $20,000, half cash and half on margin. The net result: You have lost money, and your $20,000 portfolio now consists of $10,000 cash and $10,000 you owe to the broker.

Key Point

The convenience of a margin account is accompanied by the very high risk of margin investing. You might double your capital or lose it, all very quickly.

The rule of thumb about borrowing money to invest applies to margin accounts as much as to any other form of borrowing. It is a great convenience and all too easy to use; but the risk is high if securities fall in value. This can occur very quickly and the risk is most severe when you are fully leveraged.

KNOWLEDGE AND EXPERIENCE RISK

The second kind of risk involves the combination of two things: your *knowledge and experience risk* includes your investing background as well as the collective research you have performed for yourself in the past—performing online searches and studying books, magazine articles, or annual reports.

Knowledge should be acquired from sources that make sense to you. Today, especially with so many free online organizations providing free advice, it just makes sense to verify everything. Sites that are selling something may offer claims that do not hold up.

Examples

The Road to Easy Riches: If a website wants you to subscribe to a service, make sure you know what you are going to get. If you are promised the secrets of making millions in the market or things Wall Street doesn't want you to know, it probably involves a get-rich-quick scheme that is not going to work.

Market knowledge is best acquired when it is based on the recognition of what is truly needed to succeed in any endeavor. Success is the result of hard work, study, and analysis, but no one should rely on the claims by others to having knowledge as an easy and fast way to get rich. No one is going to sell knowledge to you. Most of us know all of this already, but it is also easy to fall victim to amazing promises for a one-time payment.

margin account

An account provided to investors by their brokers, allowing them to borrow up to one-half of the value of their portfolio.

margin call

A requirement that investors deposit additional funds to meet minimum margin requirements. If the margin call cannot be met, the broker will sell some or all of the portfolio assets.

Key Point
Never believe promises of systems that make it easy to get rich. You are never going to be able to buy fast profits. However, it is quite easy to waste your money on systems that don't work.

All of the knowledge you need is out there and it is just a matter of your deciding how to acquire it. You may ask friends and relatives who have been investing for many years which books or magazines to read, which websites to visit, and how to gain solid, lasting information. You can also read reviews of books on Amazon.com or Barnes & Noble to identify the best books based on ratings and on what readers say about the books.

Experience, it has been said, often comes from making mistakes or losing money. If that is true, then losing a lot of money is *better* experience.

This does not need to be the case. In fact, you can gain experience by *paper trading* stocks before actually putting cash on the line. Paper trading is a simulation involving real-time market price movement and the selection of stocks using a fictitious fund of cash.

A word of caution: Paper trading does not involve real money so the experience you gain is going to be limited. Just as you may acquire $40,000 playing blackjack on the free Yahoo! games site, when it comes to really putting $1,000 on a single hand, most conservative people will not do it. So by the same argument, don't deceive yourself into thinking that paper trading gives you real-world experience even though the decisions you make are going to be tracked based on the real market. At some point, you are going to need actual experience, meaning actual money will have to be invested in shares of stock.

paper trading

A system of simulated investing in which a portfolio of cash can be used to buy shares of stock based on actual value in the current stock market. However, because it is a simulation, there is no risk. The purpose of paper trading is to demonstrate to a new investor how the markets work.

Paper trading is an excellent way of learning the mechanics of trading stocks, finding out how margin borrowing works, and managing the payment and delivery of shares once an order has been entered. However, there is no substitute for the real thing. You can learn the theory of riding a bicycle by studying user manuals and watching films, but you do not actually learn until you get on the bicycle for real. The same is true for gaining investing experience.

Valuable Resource
The following websites offer free paper trading:

Wall Street Survivor
   www.wallstreetsurvivor.com/home.aspx#1
Investopedia
   http://simulator.investopedia.com/Default
   .aspx?viewed=1
Stock Paper Trading
   www.stockpapertrading.com

Key Point
Paper trading is a good way to become familiar with how the mechanics of investing work. But you can never appreciate the exposure to risk in the market until your money is on the line.

The risk associated with knowledge and experience is potentially quite high. If an investor makes decisions without understanding exactly what is taking place or how prices move, then the risk exists because of a lack of knowledge and experience. So the risk of making ill-informed decisions will lead to losses. Even worse, if a lucky but ill-informed decision results in a profit, an inexperienced investor may easily decide that it makes sense to place more money at risk, leading to large losses in the second or third trade.

SECTOR RISK

A *sector* is a segment of the market that is focused on one industry. Sectors include companies that share distinct product or service attributes or serve a particular market. Here are some examples:

Sector	Industries
Agriculture	farm and construction machinery; farm products
Banking	regional; foreign regional banks; money center banks; foreign money center banks
Capital Goods	business equipment; industrial equipment and components; industrial electrical electrical equipment; aerospace and defense-major diversified; pollution and treatment controls; machine tools and accessories; fabrication; diversified machinery; small tools and accessories

The concept of *sector risk* relates to the cyclical and industrial risks each sector is vulnerable to or likely to suffer from in the event of negative economic conditions.

Sector risk comes from the natural supply and demand cycle, economic conditions and their changes, political trends and actions, and perceptions among investors about specific sectors and industries.

POLITICAL AND ECONOMIC RISK

disruption risk

The risk that trading in stocks may be disrupted by political or economic causes, acts of war, or natural disasters.

The risks associated with each sector and its industries are derived from many outside sources. Among these is *political and economic risk*, which are among the most important outside factors in assessing both the viability and value of a company, and identifying the timing of purchasing shares.

A closely related risk involves potential disruption of markets. So *disruption risk* may be a secondary fallout of either political or economic risk.

Examples of possible disruptions may include terrorist attacks that close down exchanges; power outages; catastrophic threats like pandemics, hurricanes, or flooding; or localized disruptions from labor strikes, regulatory enforcement actions, or even excessive price changes in the market. The exchanges employ stopgap measures on individual securities or even on the entire market if and when trading volatility exceeds specified levels.

Key Point

In cases of extreme price declines, exchanges will temporarily halt trading in a stock or, when the whole market is affected, on all stocks.

A trading disruption occurs in a specific security by way of a temporary suspension called a *trading halt* when news announcements that are pending are likely to create an imbalance. Examples include pending mergers or acquisitions, stock split announcements, or negotiations between companies concerning major news or consolidation or sell-off of major divisions.

A market-wide disruption can be put into motion automatically. The so-called *circuit breaker* is a programmed temporary suspension of all trading on exchanges due to exceptionally large price declines, or panics, threatening to create *liquidity risk* in the market. The halt may remain until the close of business for one session, or for a matter of hours only. The New York Stock Exchange (NYSE) identifies three possible circuit breakers at 10 percent, 20 percent, and 30 percent price declines.

With the disruption risk in mind, especially when it develops to prevent loss of liquidity, a threat of lost liquidity—or liquidity risk—arises unexpectedly and poses a serious threat to an otherwise smoothly operating market system. In some markets, liquidity is quite low and poses a different kind of threat.

trading halt

The temporary suspension of trading in a particular security in anticipation of an imbalance that may be created by upcoming announcements of mergers or acquisitions, or negotiations between companies.

Examples

What *Limited* Partner Really Means: In the limited partnership market, the lack of a secondary market for units of partnerships may mean that investors wanting to sell will have to accept a deep discount. This occurs when there is no public auction market for those units. For publicly listed shares of stock, the exchanges are usually very liquid. Any shares of stock can be efficiently and easily bought and sold at the prevailing price. This transaction can occur at any time during the trading session and a growing market in after-hours trading extends not only trading, but liquidity as well.

INFLATION RISK AND TAX RISK

Two forces—inflation and taxes—might not seem related but, in fact, they are. And together they directly influence your investment profits. The first, *inflation risk*, is your exposure to higher prices. As inflation rises (meaning everything costs more money) your capital loses its *purchasing power*. This is a huge and eroding influence on your money.

circuit breaker

An automatic halt to trading in all listed securities on exchanges, triggered by exceptionally large price declines and set to last a specified number of hours or until the end of trading for the session.

Examples

The Dwindling Dollar: To match the spending power of $100 in 1950, you would have needed $891 in 2009 just to match the purchasing power of that original $100.

liquidity risk

In the public exchanges, the possibility that high volume will curtail the availability of cash needed to complete trades in shares of stock.

inflation risk

The risk of losing purchasing power in money as a consequence of rising prices over time; for investors, inflation requires ever-higher returns on investment to offset the effects of inflation.

> **Valuable Resource**
> To calculate the spending power of any amount between any two years, go to **www.measuringworth.com/ppowerus.**

The effects of inflation are serious because as it rises, you need to earn a higher level of profits just to break even and maintain purchasing power. This translates to the demand for taking higher risks as a response to inflation. If you are so adverse to market risk that you keep your money in a safe but low-yielding account, then you lose purchasing power.

> **Examples**
>
> **Losing by Gaining:** In 2010 inflation was averaging about 2 percent. If you put your money into a certificate of deposit yielding only 0.75 percent over three months, you lose 1.25 percent of your money in reduction of purchasing power. You need to earn at least 2 percent just to match inflation—and that is before you consider the effect of taxes on your profits.

Taxes come off the top of your earnings and only make it necessary to earn higher rates of return just to meet inflation. So *tax risk* is the threat that with part of your earnings going to federal and state income taxes, the remainder, or after-tax return, will not match inflation.

The tax burden is not only federal, but has to include the state tax liability as well. When both federal and state taxes are added together, the taxable percentage can rise as high as 50 percent or more.

> **Valuable Resource**
> To find your applicable state income tax rate, go to **www.taxfoundation.org/taxdata/show/228.html.**

Valuable Resource
To find the current rate of inflation, check the BLS website at **www.bls.gov/cpi.**

So both inflation and taxes play a part in identifying the scope of risk. To maintain after-inflation and after-tax purchasing power of your capital—without even considering a true net profit—you need to calculate the effects of both. Your *break-even rate* is the rate of return you need to make just to keep your purchasing power level.

To calculate the break-even rate, first estimate the rate of inflation you expect to experience over the next year. For this, you may refer to the federal website for the Bureau of Labor Statistics (BLS), which calculates and publishes the Consumer Price Index (CPI), the usual measure of inflation. The inflation rate is divided by the percentage of income remaining after you deduct the *effective tax rate* from 100.

Examples
The Double Whammy: If your combined federal and state tax effective tax rate is 44 percent, then the calculation involves deducting 44 percent from 100 percent; the answer is 56 percent.

When you divide the assumed inflation rate by the net percentage remaining after deducting your tax rate from 100 percent, the result is the return you need to earn to break even after inflation and taxes:

$$I \div (100 - E) = B$$

In this formula, I is inflation; E is effective tax rate; and B is the break-even return. So if you assume a 2 percent inflation rate over the coming year and your combined federal and state effective tax rate is 45 percent, your breakeven is:

$$2\% \div (100 - 44) = 3.6\%$$

This shows that you will need to earn 3.6 percent net on your portfolio to maintain your purchasing power. In real terms, earning this rate does not produce any real profits; it only maintains the value of your capital.

purchasing power

The value of money when compared between years. As inflation rises, the dollar loses its purchasing power compared to past years.

tax risk

The risk that after-tax return on investment will fall short of the return needed to preserve spending power after inflation.

break-even rate

The rate of return needed from investing activity to absorb inflation and taxes, in order to maintain the purchasing power of investment capital.

effective tax rate

The rate of taxes assessed on taxable income, combining both federal and state rates.

Key Point
If you earn less than your break-even rate (after inflation and taxes), you are losing money on your investments. You will have to accept higher risks just to maintain your purchasing power.

With these assumptions, that 0.75 percent certificate of deposit is not going to be enough. You are losing purchasing power every year as long as you do not make at least the break-even rate.

The higher your tax bracket and the higher the current rate of inflation, the more difficult it becomes to break even. This is the true meaning of the combined inflation and tax risk. It may be impossible to beat inflation and taxes while also adhering to the market risk standards you set for yourself.

FUNDAMENTAL RISK

One form of risk that is not often discussed in risk terms is fundamental risk. This is the danger that the financial statements and reports issued by a corporation might be inaccurate and even deceptive.

Is this type of risk a serious one? In recent years, many investors have lost large amounts of capital due to intentional deception. The well-known case of Enron (among many other companies) involved not only intentional deception, but the willing participation of what should have been an independent auditing firm.

The rules governing how the numbers get reported are complex and al-low companies leeway in how to interpret and report numbers. Financial results do not have any one interpretation, unfortunately, because many estimates are involved for setting up reserves, placing value on inventory, and the timing of when transactions are recognized (placed onto the books). Under the accrual accounting system, all income is supposed to be recognized in the year it is earned, even though cash may not change hands until the following year. All costs and expenses are supposed to be recognized in the year incurred, even if payment is not made until the following year.

Key Point

Companies can and at times do distort their profit picture. Some distortions are legal under the accounting rules, so you need to track the trends over many years to get a grasp on the long-term growth curve.

This system is intended to ensure that the recognized revenue, costs, and expenses accurately reflect what happens each year. Because it is complex and involves estimates, it also lends itself to many liberal or aggressive decisions. Even worse, it is possible for companies to manipulate the reported outcome to make matters appear better than they are. This is what happened in Enron in the extreme.

There are many ways that companies can manipulate results, including:

- Exaggerating the current's year's revenues (reporting income that will not be earned until the following year).
- Deferring the current year's costs or expenses (setting these up as assets and then depreciating them over several years).
- Overvaluing or undervaluing inventory, bad debt reserves, and other accounting matters that have to be estimated.
- Delaying the reporting of one-time large losses.
- Changing the timing for recognition of the purchase or sale of a company or segment.

Some of these kinds of adjustments are not outright fraud but matters of interpretation. But there is a line between aggressive accounting and deception, and that line is not always easy to see in advance.

For investors who rely on the financial statements and earnings reports published by companies in order to make the decision to buy shares, the possibility that the basic information is not reliable is very troubling. The way to overcome this risk is to set standards for how you evaluate a company. These standards should include:

1. Check the numbers over as many as 10 years and look for consistent trends. When you cannot find those trends, investigate further.
2. Don't check only one or two indicators on the financial statements. Perform comprehensive analysis and compare trends in total rather than separately.
3. Consider the reputation of management as part of the equation of trust. Rely on management that has been around for a long time, in a company that has an impeccable reputation.
4. If something doesn't look right, don't ignore it. Rely on your instincts and question anything that looks out of line.

None of these four steps guarantees that you can always avoid fundamental risk. But as a general rule, if a company's stock is rising quickly and its revenue and profits continue to outpace the past year, a healthy degree of skepticism is in order. Outright fraud is rare, but aggressive accounting can be just as damaging even if it is legal. As long as everything continues to just get better, aggressive accounting is accepted by stockholders; but as soon as the market slows down, the more aggressively interpreted financial results tend to fall quickly as well.

LOST OPPORTUNITY RISK

The final type of risk to be aware of is the risk that all of your capital will be tied up in positions and you will miss new opportunities as a result. The *lost opportunity risk* is a matter that virtually all investors face and have to make decisions to deal with or overcome.

This risk comes about in several ways. In its most basic form, it exists whenever available capital is limited. Even if you employ your broker's margin account, if you cannot free up capital to invest in more positions than you hold right now, it is possible that many opportunities will come and go.

A more severe form of lost opportunity risk occurs when you sell off holdings once they become profitable, but hold onto depreciated stocks. Of course, you hope those stocks will rebound and become profitable in the future; but when you take profits, you inevitably end up with a portfolio full of stocks that have fallen in value. A solution is to match up winners and losers.

risk tolerance

The degree of risk appropriate to each individual based on experience and knowledge, available capital, income, and willingness or unwillingness to take chances.

Examples

Tax Planning to Use Losses: If two of your holdings offset each other, sell them both and free up the total to invest elsewhere. If you have a profit of $3,000 in one position and a loss of $2,500 in another, by selling them both you free up more capital and you reduce your taxable income this year by offsetting profits and losses.

Risks are best managed by setting risk-related goals. Your *risk tolerance* has to define investments that are appropriate for you based on your experience, available capital, income, and perceptions about the market.

If you do not want to risk loss, the defining phase of setting up your portfolio should be undertaken with one eye on the double effects of inflation and taxes. Settling for an exceptionally low return to avoid risk can easily lead to losses in terms of deterioration in purchasing power. It may be necessary to create a diversified risk to overcome the break-even level, but without accepting too much risk on your entire portfolio.

The next chapter expands on the discussion of how to select appropriate investments by exploring the concept of value for long-term growth of stocks in your portfolio.

THE ADVENTURES OF STOCKMAN

STOCK MAN LOOKS THROUGH THE FINANCIAL NEWS EVERY DAY TO PREPARE HIMSELF AND HIS *TRUSTY SIDEKICK* TO ONCE AGAIN TAKE ON THE MARKET FORCES, THOSE BULLS AND BEARS THAT LEAD EVERY DAY'S MARKET SESSION.

THE RISKS ARE GREAT.

TO BE CONTINUED...

3 VALUE INVESTMENT AND GROWTH INVESTMENT

The way you select investments ultimately determines how successfully you will manage your portfolio and create future profits. The concept of *value investing* appeals to many people, especially the more conservative, because it bases decisions on analysis of the basic financial strength of a company, combined with the search for bargain prices of shares. This is the equivalent of buying a car by comparing ratings and performance, and then looking for an attractive discount. The alternative—buying a car based solely on its appearance—is a popular but less successful method.

The alternative, based on predicting the future and then trying to find companies most likely to grow into the assumed scenario, *might* succeed but it is much less scientific than applying the principles of value investing. The technique of trying to anticipate the future is flawed in the sense that such assumptions are rarely accurate. It may also ignore or overlook some of the basic facts about a company's financial strength, competitive position, product or service trends, and economic forces that are going to affect future value.

value investing

A method for picking long-term investments by determining their true value and quality, and then seeking discounted prices to find bargains.

Key Point
Seeking investments conforming to assumptions about the future may ignore the basic facts about a company's strength or growth potential.

Those who try to pick investments based on assumptions about the future may actually outnumber value investors, whose emphasis is on analysis of financial fact rather than an attempt to predict future valuation and stock pricing. Value investing does not require you to predict the future or to be concerned with a variety of unknown influences on future prices. The decision to buy a particular company's stock is based on a study of current value, a history of growth, and application of a few sound fundamental principles (see Chapter 4). Returning to the analogy of the car buyer, a value investor goes to the dealership armed with comparative price and performance data, model comparisons and prices, and a very solid idea of the model and price desired. The decision is made ahead of time that if the price is available, they will buy; if that price is not available, they will wait.

The more impulsive car buyer goes to the dealership with little or no information other than what they might have heard about the brand. They end up buying for reasons that make no sense to the value investor. For example, they might buy a red car because it looks so nice—without considering the ratings, price, or performance issues.

For stock investors, the same principles apply. Value investors focus on individual companies, review the history of growth, read the annual reports, and decide in advance what is a fair price per share of the stock. It is simple and logical, but it requires more work. Once the true value of a company has been determined, the value investor will look for a buying opportunity. This means they will buy stock in the targeted company only if they can execute an order *below* the fair value price.

Do bargains arise in the market? Some theories claim that the current price of a share of stock is either efficient or random. (See Chapter 14.) An efficient price is one that has already factored in all known information about the company, meaning the price is always fair and accurate. A random price is one that changes without any prediction and may move up or down for reasons that cannot be known in advance.

Key Point

If the market were either efficient or random, it would be a 50–50 proposition to ever buy stocks. Under those theories, the current price of stock is always right or arbitrary.

Both of these theories are simply wrong. The market is anything but efficient. In fact, the inefficiencies of the market create many bargains. The market as one entity overreacts to all news, both good and bad, meaning prices tend to move too high on good news and fall too low on bad news. These jarring price changes tend to self-correct within a few trading sessions; but once they have fallen, bargains are created in a window of opportunity.

Valuable Resource

An extended discussion of the efficient market hypothesis can be downloaded at **www.vixek.com/Efficient%20 Market%20Hypothesis%20and%20its%20Critics%20 -%20Malkiel.pdf.**

Valuable Resource

To see a detailed explanation of the random walk theory, go to **www.chicagobooth.edu/faculty/selectedpapers/ sp16.pdf.**

Few people accept the idea that the pricing of stocks is random. Many reject the principles followed by value investors, noting that financial information is always out of date by the time it is published. However, current news about products, earnings, and market perceptions all affect the value of stock very specifically. Rather than believing in the random approach to value, it makes more sense to recognize that there are many things affecting price, some canceling one another out and others confirming the current *trend*.

trend

The established direction or movement of price, or changes in an indicator, that define a company's value over many months or years.

Always remember the distinction between a technical trend (price movement) and a fundamental trend (changes in profitability, working capital, or financial strength). These are not the same, although they can be used together in the analysis of companies and their stocks. However, even a consistent trend does not mean that short-term markets are efficient by any means. In the long term, a value investment is likely to be efficient in the sense that properly selected companies will experience growth. In the short term, however, the market is extremely inefficient and chaotic.

Key Point

Seeking investments conforming to assumptions about the future may ignore the basic facts about a company's strength or growth potential.

The theories concerning the efficiency of the market or its random nature are comforting to those looking at the market academically. But for people investing real money in shares of stock, these theories are either deceptively comforting (efficient at all times) or depressingly fatalistic (hopelessly random). Neither theory is realistic. The good news is that by applying the concepts of value investing, you can find value and a bargain price. It demands research and patience, but it is one way to build a profitable long-term portfolio. Two precepts every value investor has to be able to accept are:

1. Inactivity in a stock's price is not a negative attribute.
2. The market rewards patience.

It could take months, and in some cases years, for a stock's value to prove out the theory behind value investing. It is tempting to pay attention to the daily up-and-down changes in a stock's value, but that is not the way to preserve capital, avoid fast losses, or time decisions well. Value investors are patient and are willing to put in the time to research and analyze a company before buying shares.

VALUE INVESTING AND CONTROL

Using the principles of value investing to select companies and their stocks is based on a few important rules:

- Base decisions on a study of the fundamentals (see Chapter 5). Anyone can grasp and master a few important fundamental indicators and trends.
- Compare companies to rank their quality.
- Be aware of price swings and *volatility*.
- Remember to include *dividend yield* in your analysis.
- Once you buy, don't worry about price changes; remember, the market rewards patience.

How many people truly buy stocks and manage their portfolios based on these simple but practical guidelines? Not many do, unfortunately. It is far more likely that investors, even those who define themselves as fundamental or conservative in their approach, tend to take the easier path of picking stocks impulsively. Someone tells a friend or relative, "You should buy this stock. It's going to double in value in the next six months." A common reaction is to immediately buy shares, but *without knowing why*.

Key Point

Many investors buy stocks on advice from others, but may not know why that is supposed to be a good idea.

volatility

The degree of price change within a defined period of time, used as a measurement of market risk in a particular stock.

dividend yield

The return on dividends paid. To compute the annual dividend yield, divide annual dividends per share by the current price per share; the result is expressed as a percentage.

An intelligent approach would be to respond with a question: "What criteria did you use to reach that conclusion?" In other words, *why* will the stock double in value and *how* do you know that? You will find that the person giving you the advice either has no criteria to rely upon, or has based the conclusion on a simplistic indicator. For example, the company has been growing at double-digit rates, it is about to introduce a new product, or it is going to benefit from new federal legislation. Those factors might influence stock value, but they do not guarantee anything.

Under the value investing approach, you have control when you apply the rules above and when you ask a series of your own questions:

- Is the stock currently fairly valued, overvalued, or under-valued?
- What criteria determine this conclusion about valuation?
- Is this company dominant in its industry?
- What is the recent price history and level of volatility?

Asking these questions puts you in control. Buying stock should be approached on the same basis as that used to buy a home. A diligent home shopper looks at many homes and compares prices and features. The decision should not be made rashly or without completely researching the local market, neighborhood, construction quality, and fairness of the price being asked. However, when buying stocks, the same careful homebuyers might make decisions impulsively and without any research at all. That is a mistake.

VALUE INVESTING MYTHS AND FACTS

The power of value investing is in the control that people take over their own investment decisions. Rather than relying on unsupported claims or promises offered by others, or thinking of the market as a gamble, value investors are able to list out the reasons to buy stock, find companies meeting the requirements, and then act.

Key Point
Value investing places full control in your hands; taking any other approach relinquishes control, either to someone else or to the luck of the draw.

There are a few myths and misconceptions about value investing worth examining and dispelling. These include:

- *Value investing is based on a study of fundamentals, and fundamentals are expensive and difficult to understand.* In fact, with the Internet now a dominant force in the market, a vast amount of great, free information is available to everyone. A little bit of study and research proves that using a few well-selected fundamental indicators is not complicated.

   Much of the information you need can be found in a company's annual report or quarterly financial statement, both of which are usually found on the corporate website. All of the financial indicators you need can be found on a broker's free research links.

Valuable Resource
Charles Schwab & Co. (and several other online brokerages) gives its investors free access to the **S&P Stock Reports**, which are valuable sources for 10 years of fundamental information.

- *The key to value investing is getting stock at low prices.* This is not the case. The price itself is not the key; it is the price versus the value of the company. You would not want to overpay for a new home or for a car, and so you shop and compare prices. Value investors do the same thing with stocks. It is not the price per share that matters, but how that price compares to the true value of the company.

A stock worth $15 per share could be overpriced based on an analysis of the fundamentals; and a stock priced at $80 per share could be a bargain. The price per share is a relative value, and value investing is not simply a matter of buying low-priced stocks.

- *The stock market cannot be beaten with any system, not even with value investing.* A pessimistic outlook is built from the way that people invest. If you take that hot tip and buy into a company without checking anything for yourself, you probably cannot beat the stock market. It is quite unlikely that a free hot tip is also going to work out profitably for you.

  In comparison, value investing is designed specifically to enable you to eliminate riskier choices, narrow down to a few stocks that meet your criteria, identify when you will sell as those criteria change, and make a decision based on analysis rather than on chance. With value investing, you have the best chance for beating the stock market.

- *Financial statements are too complicated unless you have a degree in finance or accounting.* The belief in the complexity of financial statements is true in one respect: To follow and interpret footnotes, especially those concerned with accounting valuations and highly technical matters, does require a great deal of expertise. However, for making investment decisions, you are going to be more concerned with *financial ratios* than with the details of the statements themselves.

- These ratios are found on the research services supplied by brokerages and, in fact, are not easily found on the financial statements. The 10-year summary of key financial indicators is of far greater interest than statements themselves, and much easier to find and use.

- *Growth stocks provide better returns than value stocks.* The popularity of growth stocks cannot be ignored. A *growth stock* is one expected to report earnings above the average of all stocks, which should translate to a rapidly growing stock price as well. Growth and value stocks have each prevailed in the market about equally. However, a danger in growth stocks is that they tend to outperform the market during big growth spurts, but to fall hard and fast when they end. The dot-com bubble was one such example of growth stock domination followed by a collapse. Over the long term, value stocks compete with growth stocks equally, but are less likely to crash.

financial ratios

Tests of related financial data including operating results for a period of time (usually one full year), or the working capital and capitalization status as of a specified date (usually year-end).

Setting Standards for Buying (and Selling)

With an impulsive method for buying stocks, you cannot know when to sell. By establishing a clear set of criteria for how and when to get in, you also can monitor those standards and, if and when they change, know when it is time to sell.

Key Point

Setting criteria for buying also defines criteria for selling. Without the first step, you cannot know when or why to sell.

growth stocks

Stocks of companies expected to report better-than-average earnings and to experience rapid stock price growth as a result, at least for the period in which the growth industry remains in an uptrend.

Value investors differ from all others in the sense that they set a number of important rules for how and when to buy. If the status of a company changes, the value investor is supposed to sell the stock. So it is a disciplined approach based on defining and seeking value and keeping the position as long as the company keeps meeting the criteria.

The selection criteria begin with an observation about the short-term and long-term market. In the short term, prices change based on company popularity, fads, rumors, and overreaction to all news. This chaos tells you that trading in and out of positions is a difficult game because you need to time decisions on both sides with near-perfect precision. The swings in price are not consistent, and the chaotic nature of the short-term market points to the importance of a long-term perspective.

In the long term, stock prices tend to move in line with the company's earnings. It's really that simple. If you want to identify a company that represents value, look to past earnings trends and determine whether those trends will continue into the future. Companies that see falling sales tend to also experience falling stock prices. For examples, check General Motors, Eastman Kodak, and any large U.S.-based airline from the 1990s through to today.

These four rather obvious (but often overlooked) facts point to the first criterion of value investing:

1.   Track earnings trends to find value companies.

Another interesting fact about the market is that industries and companies experience popularity cycles. At certain times, the market is in love with one kind of company, whether that makes sense or not. At other times, the market ignores an entire industry. Value investors look for the company in an out-of-favor sector that has strong fundamentals but is not on many lists of stocks to buy.

The reason for buying an out-of-favor company is that it is probably undervalued, but assuming the cyclical nature of most sectors and also assuming that the cycle will come around again, a second criterion for value investing is:

> 2. **Look for fundamentally strong companies in sectors that are currently out of favor in the market.**

The third rule is that you want to limit your short list to companies that have excellent reputations for quality of management, for product, and for competition. A value company is most likely to dominate its industry and has dominated for many years. By definition, this domination is the result of providing value products or services, and working through exceptionally skilled management.

The third value investing rule is:

> 3. **Narrow your list down to companies that offer exceptionally high-quality products or services, are managed expertly, and dominate their industry.**

A fourth market reality is that even if prices are set efficiently most of the time, there are times when prices are pushed downward to unreasonably low levels. A company's earnings might be lower than analysts expected, even if they represent record earnings for the company. It's irrational, but it is a fact of life. Bargains show up in the market all of the time because of the short-term irrationality of buyers and sellers.

tangible book value

The net capital value of a company (assets minus liabilities) further reduced for all intangible assets. When the tangible value is divided by outstanding shares of stock, the result is the tangible book value per share.

With this in mind, you can look for bargain-priced stock when those prices fall in an exaggerated fashion. This assumes that you first qualify the company based on fundamental strength, exceptional quality, and competitive position within the company's sector. If you have done that, the fourth rule for value investing is:

> 4.   **Identify companies you consider exceptionally well managed, that dominate their industries. Then buy on dips that create bargain stock price levels.**

These four standards come down to the central definition of value investing: the selection of stocks in exceptionally well-run companies, available at a price below fair value. The definition of fair value (at times also called intrinsic value) varies. In general, it refers to stocks priced below *tangible book value* or some other assumption of value based on fundamental analysis. This may also be affected by an exceptionally attractive dividend yield available at the time the purchase is made.

Key Point
Setting criteria for buying also defines criteria for selling. Without the first step, you cannot know when or why to sell.

In comparison, growth stocks tend to rise during volatile markets moving quickly to the upside. But there is a danger. Those same stocks tend to lose value rapidly when the uptrend ends, especially if it is driven by a temporary fad in the market dominated by those industries where growth stocks are found. Consider, for example, the cyclical rise and fall in technology and IT sector stocks.

This does not mean that value stocks insulate your portfolio from price declines. But well-selected value stocks do tend to outperform the market as a whole over the long term. Within that long term it is likely that some years will be low-volume and low-growth years for value stocks. However, as a rule, value investing is more conservative and more profitable than speculation or trying to find the next growth stock.

A second source of returns on a portfolio, beyond price appreciation of stock, is dividend income. Most growth stocks do not pay dividends, so growth stock investors have to rely on price appreciation that outpaces not only the change in value investments, but their dividend yields as well. Value investors can make the most of dividend yield by reinvesting dividends in the purchase of additional shares rather than taking payments in cash. The *reinvested dividends* appreciate at compounded rates. Over many years, dividend income on value investments represents a significant share of overall returns on the portfolio, and may also be thought of as offsets to the cyclical price declines that occur in all markets.

The value investor is probably more conservative and more concerned with volatility than growth investors. However, when your emphasis is on how a portfolio is going to perform over many years and not just over the next few weeks or months, value investing is likely to be a more profitable strategy in the market.

reinvested dividends
Those dividends used to automatically purchase additional shares of stock as opposed to taking payments in cash. Reinvested dividends earn the dividend yield at a compounded rate because future dividend payments are based on the total shares held, including shares purchased with quarterly dividends.

4 MARKET STRATEGIES

Every investor needs to develop a series of strategies for investing. An *investment strategy* is a set of rules and procedures you use to pick investments, decide when to close positions, and match desired returns with levels of risk.

Investing without a specified set of rules and procedures is not advisable. You need to know what is an acceptable risk and how you are going to manage that risk through a range of selections in your portfolio. Many novice investors focus only on finding stocks they believe will increase in value. The concept of investing in this approach is summarized in a single idea: Buy stock, wait for it to grow in value, and then sell.

Key Point
Finding stocks with appreciation potential is not enough. You also need to limit your search to stocks with acceptable levels of risk.

Of course, everyone wants to make a profit. But without an investment strategy, how do you know which stocks to buy and which are too risky? How long will you hold stocks? What rate of return do you expect, or what dollar amount of profit will generate a sale? These are basic questions, but if you do not ask them, then you have not defined acceptable risks, appropriate stocks, or procedures for selling when the time is right.

A BASIC STRATEGY: BUY AND HOLD

The first and best-known market strategy is called *buy and hold*. Under this plan, you decide which stocks meet your risk criteria and are fundamentally sound, pay an attractive dividend, and are in a sector you believe has exceptional growth potential. You then buy shares of stock, intending to hold them for the long term. Properly selected value investments are likely to work best in a buy-and-hold strategy.

A buy-and-hold strategy may involve purchase of additional shares in the future, reinvestment of dividends, and well-planned diversification to avoid unnecessary market and cyclical risks.

If you combine the standards of value investing with a buy-and-hold strategy (often thought to be part of the same investment strategy), you will probably seek companies that pay a higher-than-average dividend, that are leaders in their sectors, and that have at least a 10-year record of exceptional performance under a short list of fundamental indicators (see Chapter 5).

Examples

Buy Low, Hold Long? Your portfolio contains many well-valued stocks. Because you applied sound fundamental analysis in the selection of these issues, your intention is to hold for the long term. Criteria include growing earnings, exceptionally high dividend yield, low historical volatility, steady debt ratio, and a P/E ranging between 15 and 25. However, you also have self-imposed rules for disposing of stocks. These rules are based on movement of trends outside your well-defined parameters for the buy-and-hold strategy.

Buy and hold tends to define an entire portfolio. Investors who are more conservative than average in their approach to portfolio management are likely to also be value investors. If you fit this definition, you probably will find yourself attracted to stocks that have a long history of outperforming not only the market in general, but other companies in their industry. This is one of the attributes of a value investment, and as part of the buy-and-hold approach, you are likely to be comfortable with the buy-and-hold approach to an exceptionally well managed, competitive, and adequately capitalized company.

> **Key Point**
> Value companies share many attributes, including a history of growing revenue and profits, higher-than-average dividends, and strong working capital controls.

A STRATEGIC REQUIREMENT: DIVERSIFICATION

The idea behind *diversification* is that it does not make sense to place all of your capital in one place. The risk is too great. So you spread risks by selecting different stocks or other products, so that no single economic, cyclical, or market event or news will disrupt your entire portfolio.

The methods of diversification are many. Best known among these is spreading risk by selecting different stocks. As a basic form of diversification, this move makes sense. Owning three stocks with equal dollar values in each, rather than placing all of your cash into a single stock, means that a decline in value of any one only affects one-third of the total.

The Risk of Ineffective Diversification

This may not be enough diversification, however. If all three stocks are in the same industry, a change in the economy affecting that industry is also likely to affect all three stocks. Industries tend to share the same business cycles and to react to economic news (unemployment, interest rates, currency values) in a similar manner.

Even different industries may react to the same economic news in the same manner. So simply holding several different stocks might still expose you to market risk. For example, if you hold stock in three companies, all of which do the majority of their business overseas, how will currency exchange trends affect value? If all of your companies rely on borrowing money to fund operations, how will rising interest rates impact stock prices?

To truly diversify among different companies, your holdings should be among companies that do not share the same vulnerability, especially to factors likely to hit the stock price in a negative way. For example, if you buy shares in companies in different industries but all are technology stocks, any factors hurting stock prices are likely to lead to declines in the value of your entire portfolio.

market capitalization

The total dollar value of a company's net worth, including the most frequently used classifications of large-cap, mid-cap, and small-cap.

Key Point
Owning several stocks subject to the same kinds of market risks is not diversification; it is simply living with the same risks in different stocks.

Diversifying by Company Size

Another consideration in diversifying your portfolio is the level of *market capitalization* (market cap). This is a popular comparative measurement, representing the value of a corporation's *net worth* (assets minus liabilities). Net worth primarily consists of the value of capital stock and *retained earnings*.

net worth

The dollar value of a company's equity value (assets less liabilities), divided into capital stock and retained earnings (the sum of all profits and losses from year to year) and other equity adjustments.

Market capitalization is the sum of all outstanding common shares, multiplied by the current market price per share. So when stock prices rise, so does market cap; and when market price falls, so does market cap. The distinctions are made among companies not so much due to daily price fluctuations, but in broader terms. The three primary categories in terms of market cap are *large-cap* ($10 billion or more of equity value), *mid-cap* (between $2 and $10 billion), and *small-cap* (less than $2 billion).

Additional distinctions are made by some to include *mega-cap*, or companies whose net worth is greater than $200 billion; and *micro-cap*, including companies with equity value between $50 million and $300 million.

These distinctions are important because they provide an important method for diversifying beyond simply buying different stocks. The big-cap companies are often the strongest in terms of market domination. These companies also tend to fit the definition of *blue-chip* companies, those paying dividends even in soft markets, with stable and growing earnings and little or no long-term liabilities.

In selecting large-cap stocks, you opt for safety, but at times this may also mean lower-than-average volatility. Such companies at times, but not always, may move more slowly than the average company in the market. On the other end of the spectrum, small-cap stocks tend to be much more speculative because they are young and do not have a track record. However, those that succeed may do so with dramatic price appreciation. It's important to remember that every large-cap stock started out as a small-cap stock.

Valuable Resource
A useful article on the topic of market capitalization published by Stanford University can be viewed at **www.stanford.edu/~mikefan/metrics/marketcap.html.**

retained earnings

The accumulated sum of a corporation's after-tax net profits, increased each year a profit is reported, and reduced whenever a net loss occurs.

Market capitalization as a factor in diversifying is easily overlooked but can be one of the most important ways to spread risk. It's similar to buying real estate. Where do you buy? How much are houses worth? Is the neighborhood on the rise or on the decline? Are high-priced homes appreciating faster or slower than average-priced or low-priced homes? Anyone who tracks the real estate market understands quite well how the price range of homes defines market trends. The same is true for stocks.

large-cap

A classification of companies whose total equity value is greater than $10 billion.

mid-cap

A classification of companies whose total equity value is between $2 and $10 billion.

Key Point
Large, well-capitalized companies tend to be safer. They may also tend not to offer as much profit potential. Picking the right long-term investments is a balancing act.

small-cap

A classification of companies whose total equity value is less than $2 billion.

mega-cap

Companies with equity value above $200 billion.

micro-cap

Companies with equity value of between $50 and $300 million.

A method of diversification may be to spread capital among the three major classifications (large-cap, mid-cap, and small-cap) to expose yourself to potential price appreciation while also having a portion of the portfolio in safer companies with a longer track record.

The market is huge, and you will have no problem finding companies in any of the classifications. The total value of all publicly traded companies is about $40 to $50 trillion (Reuters, March 21, 2007; and Federation of Exchanges, **www.world-exchanges.org**).

Key Point

How much is a trillion? This amount is impossible to imagine. But some perspective helps. A stack of $100 bills adding up to $1 million is about five feet high. A stack equal to $1 billion is one mile. And a stack equal to $1 trillion is 10 miles high.

Diversifying by market cap is one of many ways to spread risk. An alternative to market cap is *enterprise value (EV)*, which is a measurement of the entire business, including both equity and debt capitalization. Market cap is based on valuation of *common stock* alone; EV adds *preferred stock* as well as all long-term debt.

You can also diversify in terms of liquidation risk, meaning buying some preferred shares to create an ultra-safe position for a part of your portfolio. You may also diversify by buying some domestic and some foreign stocks. Today, with the global online availability of trading, it is easier than ever to invest around the world. Many specialized funds (see later in this chapter) also specialize by country or region. You can also diversify by investing in U.S. companies with a large share of income derived from overseas. Well-known examples include Johnson & Johnson (JNJ), Coca-Cola (KO), and McDonald's (MCD), among many others.

Mutual Funds for Diversification

Diversifying by combining direct ownership of stock and other methods is a very popular choice. The *mutual fund* has been a widely popular investment vehicle for many decades. A fund is an organization that combines the capital of thousands of individuals to create a single diversified portfolio. Funds are organized by investment objective (conservative, aggressive), type of income (growth, income), or a balance of these criteria—an income fund, for example, focused on bonds and, to a degree, on stocks paying higher-than-average dividends. A balanced fund buys positions in both equity and debt.

blue chip

Companies with strong earnings, a history of regular dividend payments, and little or no long-term liabilities; financially strong and stable companies.

Examples

Mutually Beneficial: You have devoted a segment of your portfolio to direct ownership of stocks, and another portion to mutual funds. Because you consider yourself a moderate investor, you have selected a primary mutual fund identified as focusing on *conservative growth* and a second fund identified as emphasizing *aggressive income*. This level of diversification within the realm of mutual funds is one of many methods for spreading risks.

Key Point

Mutual funds can be found to suit any investment objective and type of investment. A study of performance in all kinds of markets is an important step in selecting a fund.

enterprise value (EV)

An alternative to the measurement of value based on equity alone, or market cap; EV includes all sources of capitalization, including holders of notes and bonds (debtors), as well as common and preferred stockholders.

A variety of the traditional mutual fund is the *exchange-traded fund (ETF)*. This is a mutual fund that identifies a basket of stocks in advance and does not change that mix unless one of its components changes.

The traditional mutual fund can be bought and sold only by communicating directly with the fund's management. Value of a share of a mutual fund is determined at the end of the trading day only. In comparison, an ETF can be bought or sold on the public exchanges, and value changes during the trading day just like stock.

common stock

(Called *ordinary shares* in the UK) Ownership in a corporation including voting rights for membership on boards of directors and corporate policies. Common stockholders have the lowest priority in the event of liquidation, below bondholders and preferred stockholders.

preferred stock

Classification of ownership with priority in dividend payments and liquidation above both debtors and common stockholders; however, preferred stockholders have no voting rights.

One great advantage to the ETF beyond its high liquidity is that it identifies its components in advance, meaning the management of the fund is virtually automatic. Mutual funds charge for managing a portfolio and once you buy shares you have little to say about the buy and sell decisions management makes. In an ETF, you know in advance what is in the fund. This is an advantage because it gives you automatic diversification; it is also a disadvantage because the return on an ETF is going to be the average of all its components. For example, if an ETF holds 10 stocks in one sector, of which three outperformed the others, the overall return is going to be equal to the average of all 10, not of the three outperformers.

ETFs exist for a variety of defined groups, including:

- Specific sectors or industries
- Stocks of specific countries or regions
- Shorts (ETFs that sell components instead of buying)
- Emerging markets
- Debt instruments, including fixed-income ETFs
- Currencies
- Real estate
- Commodities

Key Point
Exchange-traded funds are the hot new kind of mutual fund. They offer many advantages, but these are no guarantee that ETFs will always outperform the traditional fund.

Every month, new ETFs are added to the growing list, and new categories are also added. The ETF market is an excellent way to diversify as long as you think the entire basket of stocks (or bonds) is worth holding. Remember, though, that an ETF will only earn the average return of all its components.

Under- and Overdiversification

This brings up a new issue concerning diversification. Clearly, the best-known problem is *underdiversification*, a condition in which you are exposed to too much risk in your portfolio because your holdings are too similar and subject to the same market forces. Equally destructive is the opposite, or *overdiversification*, when you have capital spread out so broadly that overall returns are mediocre and, worst of all, below the market average.

If you overdiversify, meaning you spread your risks around to too many different stocks, you cannot beat the market average. This is a problem faced by mutual funds, especially very large funds. They are required to limit their holdings in any one company, so they have to buy many different stocks. As a result, many are overdiversified. As a consequence, most mutual funds report results lower than the popular indexes by which the markets are measured. Only one out of six funds performed better than the bull market of the 1990s (that's only 42 out of 258 managed equity funds examined). And the average margin by which those beat the averages was very slim. (These funds were measured against the well-known S&P 500 Index.[1])

[1]John C. Bogle, *Common Sense on Mutual Funds* (New York: John Wiley & Sons, 2000).

mutual fund

An investment company designed to combine the capital of many individuals to create a single portfolio designed to meet specified investment and risk objectives.

exchange-traded fund (ETF)

A type of mutual fund with a pre-identified basket of stocks with a common element. The ETF is traded over public exchanges just like shares of stock.

Examples

Mundane Returns? You have purchased a small number of shares in dozens of companies. Your purpose was to diversify effectively. However, some of your holdings have risen in value while others have fallen. Overall, your return last year was lower than the S&P 500. What went wrong? The answer may be that you were overdiversified. A possible solution: Invest part of your portfolio in a market Index, and then focus on a very small number of exceptional companies and track their fundamentals. Buy stock in a few likely winners.

under-diversification

A common condition in which a portfolio is focused on too few stocks or on stocks exposed to the same market risks.

over-diversification

Condition when a portfolio is spread so broadly that exceptional advantages in some holdings are offset by under-performance in others, resulting in a poor overall return.

Key Point

It surprises some people to hear that most mutual funds have done worse than the market averages. This happens for many reasons, among them the tendency to overdiversify.

A more recent study, from 2004 through 2008, revealed that 66.21 percent of all managed stock funds in the United States reported results worse than the overall market (measured against the S&P Composite 1500 Index.[2])

The overall report of 66.21 percent of all funds means that only about one-third of funds outperformed the overall market. This is due to overdiversification as one important factor in the outcome. In selecting a mutual fund for those who decide to choose that route, past performance is important but so is asset size.

Diversifying with mutual funds might seem a logical and easy step. But be aware that smaller funds have greater flexibility than extremely large ones and can move money around more easily.

Buying funds is one way to diversify within the stock market. You can mix directly owned stocks with shares of mutual funds and ETFs. You can also mix between value investments and speculation, as well as stocks in between. Volatility levels are a sound test of market risk, so diversifying by levels of volatility is one final way to spread capital around.

---

[2] Justin Fox, "Breaking News: Mutual Fund Managers Keep Failing to Beat the Market," *Time/CNN*, April 20, 2009.

OTHER MARKET STRATEGIES

Diversification dominates most discussions of market strategies. You
need to spread risks while managing profits and losses, meaning constant
monitoring and rethinking of past decisions. That is the nature of investing, and in uncertain markets, diversification is essential.

Beyond the need to spread risks, additional strategies can be very useful.
Among these is *dollar cost averaging (DCA)*, a method of placing a fixed
dollar amount into the market periodically. The theory behind DCA is
that the averaging effect reduces risk and is beneficial over the long term.

Under this plan, you pay in the same amount each period (monthly,
for example). If the price per share rises, you buy fewer shares; if it falls,
you buy more shares. So you make three decisions with a DCA plan: the
amount you invest, the frequency of transfers, and the overall time period
over which the DCA plan will be made.

dollar cost averaging (DCA)

A system of investing the same dollar amount into the market periodically regardless of price changes over time, on the theory that this reduces risk.

Key Point
Dollar cost averaging is a formula for investing the same
amount periodically. It is a strategy, and there is no
guarantee that DCA investors will always make a profit.

Valuable Resource
You can search for dollar cost averaging calculators online
and make the math easier. One useful example is found at
www.buyupside.com/calculators/dollarcostave.php.

10 cows = $100

10 cows = $80

10 cows = $175

10 cows = $250

A study of what happens if the stock price moves up or down shows how DCA has appeal to many people. For example, if you transfer $500 per month into a stock currently selling at $20 per share, what happens if the stock price rises every month? An example is shown in Table 4.1.

Table 4.1 Dollar Cost Averaging, Rising Market

Month	Deposit	Share Price	Number of Shares	Average Price per Share
1	$500	$20	25.00	20.00
2	500	20.50	24.39	20.25
3	500	22.00	22.73	20.83
4	500	22.25	22.47	21.19
5	500	24.00	20.83	21.75
6	500	25.00	20.00	22.29

Notice that as the price per share increases, the average price per share tracks the uptrend, but the average is always lower than the current market price. The proponents of DCA point to this as an advantage. There is also an advantage if and when prices fall as shown in Table 4.2.

When the share price falls, the average price per share falls as well, but is always higher than current market value. So if you had bought $3,000 of stock at $20 per share in a lump sum, it would get you 150 shares. At the end of the period, it would be worth $2,400, for a loss of $600. In comparison, the approximately 165 shares would be worth $2,719, for a loss of only $281. So in a falling market, DCA reduces the market risk.

To proponents of DCA, the proof is found in a demonstration of what happens in both kinds of markets. In a rising market, the basis is always lower than the current price. In a falling market, the loss is always less than it would have been buying a lump sum at the beginning of the period.

Table 4.2 Dollar Cost Averaging, Falling Market

Month	Deposit	Share Price	Number of Shares	Average Price per Share
1	$500	$20	25.00	20.00
2	500	19.50	25.64	19.75
3	500	18.75	26.67	19.42
4	500	18.00	27.78	19.06
5	500	17.00	29.41	18.65
6	500	16.50	30.30	18.21

Key Point

The decision to invest with DCA or by lump sum is a matter of personal choice, including opinions about how rapidly price appreciation (or decline) is likely to occur.

To critics of the system, the whole DCA looks like a gimmick. A variation is to time purchases of stock for price dips. Markets rarely move straight up or down over six months, but are more likely to experience price changes in either direction. So if you buy after a significant price decline, you get a better average price. For the long-term-minded value investor, the timing of purchases seems too much like a speculative timing strategy and may easily lead to lost opportunities if the price continues to rise while the investor waits on the sideline for the price dip that never arrives.

EX-DIVIDEND DATE BUYING

Another strategy involves timing the purchase of stock right before the *ex-dividend date*. A stockholder has to own the stock prior to this date in order to earn a quarterly dividend, even though the dividend payment does not occur for up to a month later. So if you buy stock on or after ex-date, you will not earn a dividend until three months later.

Valuable Resource
A timely dividend calendar published the thestreet.com shows upcoming ex-dividend dates by date and by company. It is found at **www.thestreet.com/dividends/index.html.**

This brings up an interesting timing strategy that even value investors can employ. For example, if a company has declared a dividend of $2.20 per share, every 100 shares earns $220 per year or $55 per quarter. If you buy 100 shares before ex-date, you are entitled to that $55. The price per share may dip on ex-date to allow for this benefit, but if you have also qualified the stock as a long-term value investment, it makes sense to time your purchase in this manner.

Key Point
Timing purchase with ex-dividend date in mind increases dividend income in the first quarter the position is owned.

Why wait three months before earning your first dividend when you could earn two quarterly dividends in the same time period? This doubles your dividend income in the first three months, just by being aware of the ex-date.

A related strategy is to reinvest dividends in the purchase of additional shares, which creates a compound return rather than a simple return based on dividend yield. Most brokerage accounts allow you to make this election at the time you purchase shares.

In all market strategies, you will also want to establish clear policies and goals for buying as well as for selling shares of stock. The basic goal of buying should be based on a complete analysis of a company's fundamentals (see Chapter 5). If you wait for a price dip to buy shares, you are likely to get a short-term bounce on the price, which is a good start to a long-term hold.

ex-dividend date

The cutoff date for earning of dividends. Stockholders who own stock the day before ex-date earn a dividend to be paid a few weeks later. Anyone buying stock on or after the ex-date has to wait until the next quarter before earning dividends.

Key Point
Knowing when to buy is an important skill. However, it is equally important to know when to sell.

It is equally important to know when to sell. Long-term buy-and-hold does not mean keeping a stock in your portfolio no matter what. Value investors need to continually monitor a company to ensure that it continues to meet the criteria for a value investment. As soon as a company's fundamental strength or profitability change, it is likely that stock prices will begin to decline. Recognizing the changes as soon as they begin gives you the chance to sell shares and find a new, stronger candidate. By monitoring the fundamental trends, you will be able to spot a reversal or leveling out of those trends, and to decide right away whether to continue holding or to sell.

The next chapter examines some of the more important fundamental indicators you need to track.

TO BE CONTINUED...

CHAPTER 5 FUNDAMENTAL ANALYSIS

There are two general schools of thought concerning how to pick stocks. This chapter examines the basic nature of fundamental analysis, the examination and analysis of *financial statements* and related news and trends, and how the indicators found in the historical record are used to pick companies and then buy their stock.

The second approach is technical analysis, or the analysis of price and chart patterns to spot reversals in trends and to time the purchase or sale of stock. The technical side is the focus of the second part of the book, and the specific indicators technicians use are found in Chapter 12.

> **Key Point**
> The most important difference between fundamental and technical is in the nature of data used. Fundamentals focus on the published results of operations; technicals involve price patterns and changes.

On the fundamental side, the starting point of analysis of the most recent results of operations is found each year in the annual report. This not only summarizes the financial statements, but includes management's explanation of the financial record, markets, products, or services, and how the company plans to compete in the immediate future.

The annual report is available on the website for a *listed company*. Most provide the report in either PDF or HTML format, or the report can be requested for delivery in hard copy. This is true for nearly all of the companies whose shares are traded publicly and owned by either *institutional investors* or *retail investors*.

The annual report includes extensive narrative sections explaining the significance of the numbers found in the financial statements. However, annual reports also have three major drawbacks for the purpose of performing in-depth analysis of trends:

1. *The statements and footnotes are very technical.* It is not easy to understand many of the technical accounting explanations included in the footnotes, which at times run 100 pages or more. The complexity of the accounting narratives makes annual reports useful to only a few financial experts.

2. *The narrative explanations may be factual or marketing-related.* It is not always easy to distinguish between factual interpretations of a company's results and the promotional spin management places on what may be a weak year or even a failed year. The management explanation is always upbeat and positive, making it difficult to determine how objectively the financial results are being interpreted.

3. *The annual report, in spite of its length, lacks detail.* To properly analyze the fundamentals, you need as many years of results as possible. Annual reports may provide only three or five years' worth of selected financial results, and in some cases only the current year and the previous year. Additionally, most annual reports leave out key ratios and indicators, so that you have to study the details to create your own base for analysis.

Key Point
The annual report is a valuable source for information; but it also has limitations. You get much better information from free research services that summarize important indicators and give you many years' history.

Valuable Resource
A free service for finding annual reports for any listed company is **www.annualreports.com**. You can also download annual reports for any company if you know their trading symbol.

Need to look up a company's ticker symbol? A free online service is offered by marketwatch.com to help with this: **www.marketwatch.com/tools/quotes/lookup.asp.**

retail investors

Individuals who own shares in publicly traded companies through direct ownership (as opposed to buying shares in mutual funds).

core earnings

A calculated adjustment to net earnings to isolate earnings from the company's primary, or core business. All noncore, nonrecurring, or extraordinary items are adjusted out of the calculation of net earnings allowed under the accounting rules.

The drawbacks in annual reports are best overcome by relying on a longer-term summary of not only the key financial results, but the important indicators as well. Most online brokerage services provide members with free analytical services. One of the best of these is the S&P Stock Report, which is available for over 5,000 listed companies. This is provided free of charge to subscribers of Charles Schwab & Co., TD Waterhouse, Scottrade, and e*Trade. The S&P Stock Reports contain a wealth of information for a 10-year period. This includes not only the key information you find in the financial statements, but other information as well for 10 years, including:

- Financial ratios derived from the financial statements
- Dividend history
- P/E high and low history
- Core earnings
- Extensive narrative analysis of the corporation and its markets

The *core earnings* deserve additional explanation. Under the rules accountants use, some nonrecurring transactions are allowed to be included in net earnings. However, Standard & Poor's developed a calculation to isolate the net profit from the company's *core* or primary business. The differences between net income and *core* net income can be substantial, so this is an important additional form of fundamental information.

Examples

The Same but Different: In reviewing two companies that seem about the same in terms of fundamental criteria and trends, you notice that one has virtually no core earnings adjustments; but the other reported substantial changes between net return and core earnings. As a result, you select the one with little or no adjustments.

Key Point

Reported net income is not always the most accurate summary of what took place for the year. For that you need to track core earnings and to be aware of the changes between net and core—the bigger the changes, the less accurate the traditional fundamental indicators.

Financial statements are prepared in a well-defined but archaic format. This means that much of the valuable information you need in order to track fundamental trends is simply not available from the latest published financial statements or annual reports. This is why you will find it more convenient to make use of services like the S&P Stock Reports for 10 years of history, rather than trying to master financial statements and how they work. However, it is also important for every fundamental investor to know what financial statements contain and what they reveal.

fiscal year

The tax year used by a corporation, which may end in any quarter selected by the company. Fiscal years may correspond to the natural business cycle rather than to the calendar year.

THE BALANCE SHEET

There are two kinds of financial statements and both follow a long-standing format of reporting. So if you understand how one set of financial statements is organized, you are well suited to follow any other corporate financial statement as well.

The first of these two is the *balance sheet*. It is given this name for two reasons. First, it summarizes the ending balances of all asset, liability, and net worth accounts as of a specific date. That date is the ending date of the period being reported, usually the last day of the quarter or *fiscal year*. Second, the sum of all asset account balances is equal to the sum of liabilities plus net worth accounts.

The first component of the balance sheet is a category called *current assets*. These are all assets in the form of cash or that are convertible to cash within 12 months. Included are cash, accounts receivable, notes receivable, marketable securities, and inventory.

In order, after current assets, the next group is called *long-term* assets (also called *fixed assets*). This is the net value of all *capital assets* minus *accumulated depreciation*.

After these two categories, additional asset groups include *prepaid assets*, *deferred assets*, and *intangible assets*. Prepays or deferrals are the values of expenses properly covering more than one year, and set up for annual *amortization*, reducing the asset and transferring relevant portions to expense. Deferred assets are entire sums paid in advance but properly belonging to a future fiscal year. They are placed in the asset account until transferred to the expense category later. Intangible assets are all assets without physical value, including the assigned value of goodwill or covenants not to compete.

The asset accounts are added together to report the total of the corporation's properties, before being reduced by offsetting debts and obligations. It is important to use the subdivisions listed above, because so many ratios and indicators rely on distinctions between various asset classes.

current assets

All assets in liquid form, meaning cash or convertible to cash within 12 months.

long-term assets

The net value (basis minus accumulated depreciation) of capital assets, including real estate, autos and trucks, machinery and equipment, furniture and furnishings, and tools.

Key Point

The subcategories of financial statements are critically important. Many key ratios are based on isolated classes of accounts.

capital assets

All assets set up to be periodically depreciated because their value outlasts a single accounting year; when fully depreciated, the capital asset's book value is zero.

accumulated depreciation

The sum of all years' depreciation expense recorded and claimed. The annual expense is offset by the accumulation account, which is a negative asset, or a reduction of the book value of capital assets.

Assets are the top half of the balance sheet. On the bottom half are two main groups, liabilities and net worth. Liabilities include all of the debts and obligations (as well as any deferred credits), and net worth is the sum of capital stock, retained earnings, and other ownership accounts. Examples of *other* accounts include treasury stock, which is the value of corporate stock the company purchases on the open market and retires permanently.

Key Point
The total of all liabilities plus net worth accounts is always equal to the total of all assets, without exception.

The first group under the liabilities section is *current liabilities*. This is the sum of all debts payable within 12 months, including accounts and taxes payable and the current portion (12 months) of all long-term liabilities.

Next are the *long-term liabilities*, which are all debts owed by the company beyond the next 12 months. These include notes or contracts payable as well as the outstanding balances of bonds issued.

A final section included on this part of the balance sheet is not actually a liability, but a form of revenue received but not yet earned. All such *deferred credits* are assigned to this category. For example, a customer pre-pays a large purchase. The corporation has received the cash but it will not be earned until next year. In the current year, this is set up as a deferred credit.

The final section of the balance sheet is the net worth section. This includes capital stock and retained earnings as well as any other additional forms of net worth or adjustments. The sum of all net worth accounts is added to the sum of all liability accounts, and that total is identical to the sum of all asset accounts.

Note: How is the balance accomplished? The sum of liabilities and net worth is always equal to the value of all asset accounts because of double-entry bookkeeping. Every entry has a debit and a credit and these are equal in value. They may also be thought of as a plus and a minus. At any time, the sum of all accounts in the corporate books will add up to zero, because debits and credits offset one another.

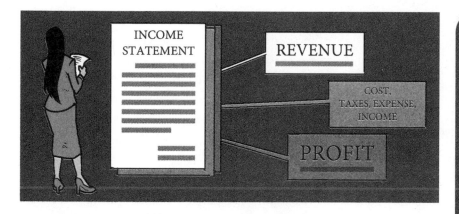

THE INCOME STATEMENT

The second type of financial statement is the *income statement* (also called profit and loss statement or statement of operations). This statement summarizes all revenue, costs, expenses, and profits for a specified period of time, such as a quarter or fiscal year.

Key Point

Like the balance sheet, the income statement is divided into distinct sections. This is crucial for analysis as well as comparisons between companies.

The income statement can be easily summarized by its major parts and subtotals:

Revenue
Minus: Cost of Goods Sold
Equals: Gross Profit
Minus: General Expenses
Equals: Net Operating Profit
Plus or Minus: Other Income and Expense
Equals: Pretax Profit
Minus: Liability for Income Taxes
Equals: Net Profit

The category of *cost of goods sold* (also called *direct costs*) includes all expenditures that are assignable directly to revenue production, including merchandise purchased, manufacturing or production labor (direct labor), freight, and the net change in inventory levels for the year.

prepaid assets

Expenses paid in one year but properly assigned to two or more years, set up as an asset to be amortized properly to future periods.

deferred assets

Expense payments made in one year but belonging completely to a future year, left as an asset until reversed and transferred in the proper accounting period.

intangible assets

Assets lacking physical value, including goodwill and covenants not to compete.

The cost of goods sold is expected to rise and fall along with revenue, and the percentage of these costs to revenue is expected to remain fairly constant. Changes may occur as a result of mergers and acquisitions, or disposal of an operating segment, when the mix of products also changes as a result.

When the cost of goods sold is subtracted from revenue, the resulting dollar value is called *gross profit*. Like the cost of goods sold, gross profit is expected to remain at about the same percentage level of revenue from year to year. This may change due to improved efficiencies, changes in inventory practices or valuation, and changes in market pricing.

Next, the expenses are deducted. These may be finely broken down into major groups such as selling expenses and general and administrative expenses (overhead), although most income statements show single values only and may explain the details through a footnote or supplementary schedule. When expenses are deducted from gross profit, the result is the *net operating profit*.

Next, other income and expenses are added or deducted. These include items such as currency exchange, one-time losses or adjustments, proceeds from the sale of capital assets, interest income or expenses, income from trading in derivatives, and all other nonoperating profit or loss. When the other income and expense net is added to or deducted from net operating profit, the result is called *pretax profit*. If other income exceeds other expense, the change will increase the net profit. If other expenses are greater, the change will decrease the net profit.

The final change is the liability for income taxes. This is deducted from the pretax profit to arrive at the final number, the *net profit* for the period.

Key Point
Financial statements all use the same basic format. This makes it easier to compare results between companies and between years.

THE P/E RATIO: FINDING A BARGAIN-PRICED STOCK

There are potentially dozens of indicators and ratios you can use to study the financial statements of a company. For the purpose of creating a basic starting point, focus here is on a very short list of fundamental indicators. These can be based strictly on the financial information you extract from the financial statements or, in one important exception, may combine financial and technical sides. This one exception is the *price/ earnings ratio (P/E)*. This is a comparison between the price per share and the reported *earnings per share (EPS)* reported most recently by the company.

The P/E ratio is a good place to start in exploring a range of fundamental indicators because it combines technical (price) with fundamental (earnings), and also because it matches dissimilar timing indicators. Price is current, whereas earnings may be as much as three months in the past and not always reflective of what is going on today.

Key Point
The P/E ratio combines technical (price) and fundamental (earnings) information to create a hybrid indicator.

Some analysts like to use *forward P/E* to analyze companies and their current earnings potential. This is a comparison between current price and estimated earnings for the coming year.

Justification for the forward P/E is that it makes the indicator more current. However, a lot of change can take place in the future, and as an indicator of stock value, forward P/E is not a reliable one. Any indicator that includes estimates should be used only cautiously.

Key Point
The forward P/E is a difficult indicator to rely upon, because it uses estimates in place of published results. The historical P/E is more reliable, when studied over a 10-year period.

long-term liabilities
All debts of a company owed beyond the next 12 months, including notes, contracts, and bonds.

deferred credits
Accounts in the liability section of the balance sheet, representing revenues received but not earned until a future period.

income statement
A financial statement summarizing revenue, costs, earnings, and profits for a specified period of time, usually a quarter or fiscal year.

In calculating the historical P/E, the current share price is divided by the latest reported EPS, or earnings per share:

$$P \div E = P/E$$

For example, if the latest reported price per share is $42.50 and the latest reported EPS was $2.85 per share, P/E (rounded up) is:

$$\$4.250 \div \$2.85 = 15$$

This calculation applies to the current price. However, given the problem with timing of the two sides of the P/E, how can this ratio be used reliably to judge a company and its stock price? The real value in fundamental analysis requires long-term trend tracking, and the P/E is no exception to this. You need to find companies with a long record of the P/E remaining within what you consider a reasonable point range. For many, this is between 10 and 25, although opinions also vary. The higher the P/E, the more expensive the stock; that is the important thing to remember.

Tracking the P/E range for a 10-year period demonstrates how the historical range of P/E from highest to lowest per year helps to find price and value stability. In Figure 5.1, the 10-year high and low P/E for General Mills (GIS) is summarized.

Notice how consistent the range has remained for the past 7 of the 10 years. The high P/E never went above 21 and the low was consistently between 13 and 15. This demonstrates a very consistent record of fair pricing for General Mills' stock.

In comparison, the 10-year record for Caterpillar (CAT) paints a different story, as shown in Figure 5.2.

In this case, the five years in the middle of the range (between 2003 and 2008)) were consistent and ranged between 17 and 12. At the end of fiscal 2010, the range was between 23 and 12, returning to a more normal range set for this company.

Figure 5.1 P/E Ratio, 10 Years: General Mills (GIS)
Source: S&P Stock Reports.

Tracking the P/E not in the moment but as a range over 10 years makes more sense, especially given the mix of technical and fundamental, and with the time disparity between current price and latest reported earnings.

pretax profit

The net profit earned for a quarter or fiscal year, before calculating the liability for income taxes; the net left when other income and expenses are added to or subtracted from net operating profit.

Figure 5.2 P/E Ratio, 10 Years: Caterpillar (CAT)

Source: S&P Stock Reports.

Key Point

When you see a sudden upward spike in the P/E, it does not mean the company is a bad investment. It does mean the current price level is probably too high and may be due for a correction.

net profit

The *bottom line*, the final profit when all adjustments and deductions have been made.

REVENUE AND EARNINGS: FUNDAMENTALS BASED ON THE OPERATING STATEMENT

The operating statement provides the second area worth detailed analysis over several years. Just as you cannot make sound judgments about the current P/E ratio without studying the longer-term trend, you cannot truly appreciate the significance of the current revenue and earnings without seeing how the trend has moved over a decade.

Tracking revenue and earnings is not just a matter of making sure that the numbers rise every year. You look for true growth, meaning that the dollar value of revenues and the dollar value of net earnings both rise each year. But you also want to see net profits maintained at a consistent or growing percentage of revenues. Even when the dollar value of earnings rises, if the percentage is declining, that is a negative sign. It probably means that costs and expenses are outpacing the growth in revenue, and that is never a positive trend.

Referring to the two previously cited companies as examples of the trend in P/E ratio, you can also track revenue and earnings trends over the same period. Figure 5.3 summarizes the General Mills (GIS) record of the operating results for a decade.

price/ earnings ratio (P/E)

A comparison between the current price per share and the latest reported earnings per share, indicating the current market perception of future earnings potential.

Figure 5.3   Revenue and Earnings, 10 Years: General Mills (GIS)
Source: S&P Stock Reports.

The dollar values of the revenue and earnings were very consistent in growing each year. The net return ranged between 9.0 percent at the earliest point to 10.3 percent at the latest year. The overall trend in revenue and earnings as well as net return was very consistent.

In comparison, Caterpillar experienced a steady improvement in net profits over the first eight years, a slight decline and then a huge drop in 2009. This occurred as the P/E shot up, as shown in the previous section. Figure 5.4 summarizes the revenue and earnings of Caterpillar over a decade.

Figure 5.4 Revenue and Earnings, 10 Years: Caterpillar (CAT)
Source: S&P Stock Reports.

Caterpillar's net return grew from 1.6 percent up to 8.7 percent in 2006, but the large drop in 2009 ended up with only a 2.8 percent net return. In 2010, net return moved back up to 6.3 percent.

This kind of analysis, coupled with a study of the P/E range each year, helps to clarify the true condition of a company and its prospects for future growth.

Key Point

Track revenue and earnings trends to spot not only dollar levels of change but net return percentages as well. Look for consistency. When you see net return falling while dollar levels rise, the trend is turning negative.

earnings per share (EPS)

The latest reported earnings, expressed as a division of earnings by the total shares outstanding during the reported year.

The study of revenue and earnings should track not only the earnings and net return in relation to sales, but also the gross profit and level of expenses. This helps to determine the causes for deterioration in net return, although the details are not always easy to find. You may need to rely on the details in annual reports to discover the reasons for the reduction in net return. Also be aware that a change in the mix of products will affect the trend. Any time a company adds an acquired competitor or sells off an operating segment, the long-term trend should be restated. If it is not, then the trend is no longer valid.

WORKING CAPITAL: FUNDAMENTALS AS A FORM OF MONEY MANAGEMENT

The final major area worth analysis is working capital. This is the amount of cash available to pay for current expenses and to fund growth and dividend payments. In its most basic definition, working capital is the net of current assets minus current liabilities. But in a broader sense, it refers to the longer-term trend reflecting the company's management of cash.

The best-known working capital test is called the current ratio. This is an indicator derived by dividing current assets by current liabilities. The outcome should be a positive value, meaning there are more liquid assets on hand than the company owes in the next 12 months. A current ratio of less than 1 is a sign of very weak cash management. The expectation of a current ratio of 2 or better means excellent cash management; but many well-managed companies maintain their current ratio somewhere between 1 and 2.

The current ratio is rounded to a whole number and one decimal place. For example, if a company reports current assets of $1,462,000 and current liabilities of $845,400, the current ratio is:

$$\$1,462,000 \div \$845,400 = 1.7$$

As with all fundamental tests, it makes sense to track current ratio for a full year. For example, in the case of General Mills and Caterpillar, current ratio over 10 years was:

Current Ratio, 10 Years		
Year	GIS	CAT
2001	0.6	1.3
2002	0.6	1.3
2003	0.9	1.3
2004	1.2	1.3
2005	0.7	1.2
2006	0.5	1.2
2007	0.5	1.2
2008	0.8	1.2
2009	1.0	1.4
2010	1.1	1.4

Both of these are consistent enough over time, although in the case of GIS, current ratio has often been below 1. However, the consistency in both companies is reassuring, if the analysis is limited to a study of only the current ratio. However, it is quite easy to manipulate this ratio by borrowing money and holding proceeds in cash. This raises the current asset level, but the offsetting liability is long-term and does not show up as a current liability (except the coming 12 months of debt service). This hides a potential problem: the rise of long-term debt. As long as the current ratio remains constant and is used as the sole test of working capital, this situation does not come to light.

Key Point

The current ratio is the best-known test of working capital, but it does not tell the whole story. The real long-term trend can only be understood by studying both the current ratio and debt ratio.

With this in mind, a second test is needed. The *debt ratio* is a comparison between long-term debt and *total capitalization*. The debt ratio is a percentage, but it is normally expressed as a value to one rounded decimal place, without percentage signs.

For example, a company reports current long-term debt of $41,200,000 and stockholder's equity of $98,600,000. Total capitalization is a combination of these two:

$$\$41,200,000 + \$98,600,000 = \$139,800,000$$

The debt ratio is found by dividing long-term debt by total capitalization. The debt ratio is:

$$\$41,200,000 \div \$139,800,000 = 29.5$$

This company is capitalized 29.5 percent by debt and 70.5 percent by equity. However, it is not the relative portion of debt or equity that is conclusive, since the levels of debt capitalization vary by industry. What is important is how the debt ratio changes over time. Whenever you see a growing debt ratio, it is a danger sign. The more long-term debt a company is obligated to repay, the worse future working capital will be. As a growing amount of annual earnings have to be paid to bondholders and note holders in interest, less is left for payment of dividends to stockholders or to fund future expansion.

An analysis of General Mills and Caterpillar for the 10-year period ending in 2010 shows how the debt ratio evolved.

Debt Ratio, 10 Years		
Year	GIS	CAT
2001	82.4	66.8
2002	57.5	67.9
2003	55.1	69.8
2004	50.3	68.0
2005	32.9	65.0
2006	21.7	72.0
2007	28.9	66.7
2008	35.4	77.2
2009	49.3	37.1
2010	41.3	27.6

In the case of General Mills, the high debt ratio at the beginning of the period was troubling, especially considering that the current ratio was less than 1 for most of the period. However, the company cut its debt ratio by nearly one-half over the decade. Caterpillar, an industry in which high debt ratios are expected, maintained a consistent level with a sudden increase in 2008 and a surprising decline in 2009. However, the consistency of the company's current ratio, coupled with the debt ratio history, indicates sound cash flow management and healthy working capital.

total capitalization

The combination of long-term debt (debt capitalization) and net worth (equity capitalization).

Key Point

It is not the debt ratio in the current year that matters, but the long-term trend. When you see the debt ratio climbing every year, it spells trouble for future cash flow.

In the selection of one stock over another, a key ingredient—but one often overlooked—is dividend income. Dividends may play a major role in overall return from your investment. The next chapter examines dividend yield and various strategies that you can employ in managing your portfolio.

TO BE CONTINUED...

6

DIVIDEND STRATEGIES

Investors tend to think in terms of capital gains, buying shares of stock and selling at a higher price. If you make $500 on a $5,000 investment, you are up 10 percent. This focus makes sense in one respect, because it's all about selling at a higher price than you bought.

However, it is easy to overlook or ignore the significance of dividend income. Dividends often represent a major percentage of overall returns, so as invisible as dividends might be, their importance should be kept in mind as you pick stocks.

DIVIDEND YIELD AS A MEANS FOR STOCK SELECTION

Even if dividend yield—the percentage you earn in dividends based on the price of stock—is used only as a means for narrowing down your list of stock candidates, it is a valuable distinction to make.

If you want to buy 100 shares of stock and you have narrowed the field down to three candidates, how do you make your decision? If all of your selection criteria are approximately equal, you still need to pick only one. The answer is to go with the best dividend yield.

Examples

Up in smoke: You have decided to invest in a tobacco company, believing that the industry is due for a big move upward. The field has been narrowed down to two companies: Altria (MO) was priced in January, 2012, at $29. Philip Morris (PM) was priced at $77. You want to invest less than $9,000 and your analysis reveals that the two both represent worthwhile candidates. You have these choices:

      300 shares of MO at $29 = $8,700
      110 shares of PM at $77 = $8,470

You decide to focus on MO, whose dividend yield was 5.66 percent. In comparison, PM's dividend was 4.00 percent. Both of these yields are exceptional. However, MO's is over 40 percent higher than PM's.

CALCULATING DIVIDEND YIELD

Dividends represent one of two possible sources of profit when you own stock. Even so, a majority of stocks—about 55 percent—pay no dividend. For many of these companies, a philosophy of management is at work. Management argues that paying dividends prevents expansion; that capital can be better used to grow the business; and that investors are not concerned with the relatively small dollar amount of a quarterly dividend. Some companies yield a small dollar value per share, and pay it out per quarter; and in terms of actual dollars, it is not much. This is debatable, especially if you become a believer in earning dividends each quarter.

Key Point

Companies have different management philosophies. Most prefer using profits for expansion and operations. Others believe investors have incentive to hold onto stock if they receive quarterly dividends.

A breakdown of 10,498 companies in terms of dividend payments is provided in Figure 6.1.

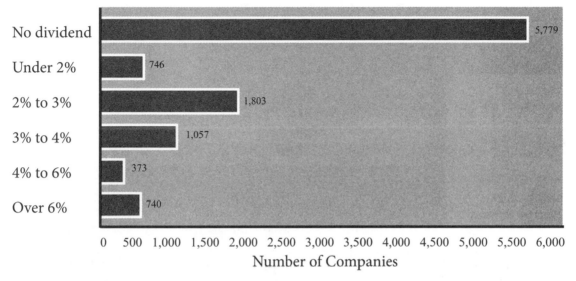

Figure 6.1 Companies Paying Dividend, by Dividend Yield
Source: Charles Schwab & Co., Stock Screener.

Although more than half of all companies pay no dividends, you may choose to invest in companies that do—and even choose to focus on those yielding better than average dividends to shareholders.

The dollar amounts may be small. However, a more reliable way to measure dividend is by the yield it represents. To calculate dividend yield, divide the dividend paid per share by the price per share; this gives you the quarterly dividend. Multiply that by four (quarters) to find the annual yield:

$$MO \quad (0.41 \div 29) \times 4 = 5.66\%$$
$$PM \quad (0.77 \div 77) \times 4 = 4.00\%$$

The dividend yield should always be applied to the price per share that you pay upon purchase. As the share price changes, so does the yield. However, your yield will always be based on what you pay, and not on what it is later after price movement.

As the stock price rises, the dividend yield falls; and as the price declines, dividend yield increases. This occurs because the dividend per share is fixed, usually for a full fiscal year. No matter what changes occur in the price, the dividend per share remains the same.

If MO's price were to range for the fiscal year between $31 and $27, yield would also change:

$$(0.41 \div 27) \times 4 = 6.07\%$$
$$(0.41 \div 28) \times 4 = 5.86\%$$
$$(0.41 \div 29) \times 4 = 5.66\%$$
$$(0.41 \div 30) \times 4 = 5.47\%$$
$$(0.41 \div 31) \times 4 = 5.29\%$$

The same changes would apply to PM. If the price ranged between $81 and $73, dividend yield would also evolve:

$$(0.77 \div 73) \times 4 = 4.22\%$$
$$(0.77 \div 75) \times 4 = 4.11\%$$
$$(0.77 \div 77) \times 4 = 4.00\%$$
$$(0.77 \div 79) \times 4 = 3.90\%$$
$$(0.77 \div 81) \times 4 = 3.80\%$$

If you bought MO at $29 per share, your dividend yield would always be 5.66 percent on those shares. The only way to change this would be to buy an additional lot at a different price and then average the two yields.

Examples

Averaging MO money: You bought 100 shares of MO at $29 per share; your dividend yield was 5.66 percent. A few months later, the share price had fallen to $27 per share. You bought another 100 shares, getting a yield of 6.07 percent. Your average price per share was adjusted to $28:
$$(\$29 + \$27) \div 2 = \$28$$
Your dividend yield is also averaged:
$$(5.66\% + 6.07\%) \div 2 = 5.865\%$$

$$\left(\frac{\text{dividend per share}}{\text{price per share}} \right) \times 4 \text{ quarters} = \text{annual yield}$$

REINVESTING DIVIDENDS

You have a choice about how dividends will be paid out to you. A relative small dollar amount may be nice, but in many instances it will just be added to the cash balance in your account. If this is the case, a dividend payment might not be significant.

> **Key Point**
> Taking dividends in cash produces a small but consistent cash addition to your portfolio. But taking dividends in additional partial shares (reinvesting) converts the dividend rate to a compounded rate.

An alternative is to reinvest dividends. Online brokerage firms provide this as a choice when you buy shares. If you choose to reinvest instead of receiving dividends in cash, you get additional partial shares. For example, if you own 100 shares and the quarterly dividend is 41 cents, you get $41 in reinvested shares. As with MO, if share price is $29 per share, the quarterly dividend will be 1.414 shares ($41 ÷ $29 = 1.414).

Systems allowing you to take advantage of this feature are called *dividend reinvestment plans (DRIPs)*. But why reinvest dividends? The answer is, by reinvesting you get a compound rate of return. Just as compound interest increases the annual stated yield, so does compound dividends.

dividend reinvestment plans (DRIPs)

features provided to investors when shares of stock are bought, allowing the choice to receive dividends in the form of additional partial shares instead of cash.

Examples

MO Compounding: You own 100 shares of MO and have received $41 in dividends this quarter. This represents 5.66 percent in dividend yield. You decide to reinvest dividends, meaning that next quarter, you will earn dividends on 101.414 shares. Taking this out for four quarters:

> 1   0.41 x 100 shares = $41.00
> $41.00 ÷ $29 = 1.414 shares, total 101.414
>
> 2   0.41 x 101.414 shares = $41.58
> $41.58 ÷ $29 = 1.434 shares, total 102.848
>
> 3   0.41 x 102.848 = $42.17
> $42.17 ÷ $29 = 1.454 shares, total 103.302
>
> 4   0.41 x 103.302 = $42.35
> $42.35 ÷ $29 = 1.460 shares, total 104.762

Over the period of one year (based on the price you paid per share of $29) you end up with an extra 4.762 shares and the annual rate will be:

(1 + 01414)4 = 5.78%

> Or:

1.01414 x 1.01414 x 1.01414 x 1.01414 = 5.78%

So if you take dividends in cash, you earn 5.66 percent, but if you reinvest in additional partial shares, your compounded dividend yield is 5.78 percent per year.

WHEN DIVIDENDS ARE EARNED AND PAID

As an investor, you face a number of important dates related to dividends. In order to properly time both purchase and sale of stock, you need to be aware of these dates and how they affect your dividend earnings.

Key Point

Dividends are not paid on the same day they are earned. Given the volume of exchanges of shares of stock, it may take as much as a full month before a company makes payment to stockholders of record.

The first date is called the declaration date. This is the date that the company's board of directors declares its intention to pay a dividend. The declaration includes specifying the ex-dividend date, record date, and

DECLARATION EX-DIVIDEND RECORD PAYMENT

payment date. It also specifies whether dividends are to be paid quarterly or in some other method (semi-annually or annually). The declaration normally applies for an entire fiscal year, so if quarterly dividends are to be paid, these dates would be set for all four quarters.

Second is the ex-dividend date. This is the cut-off date for earning dividends. If you own stock the day before the ex-dividend date, you will earn the current dividend. If you do not buy until on or after (or if you sell before) then you will not earn a dividend in the current quarter. When you qualify for the dividend, the status is also called *cum dividend*, which means "with dividend."

The third important date is called record date. This is the official date when ownership is set for the purpose of owning a dividend. It falls two business days after ex-dividend date. This is the time required for settlement. So if you buy stock before the ex-dividend date, the transaction settles three days later.

Finally, the payment date is the date when dividends will be paid, either in cash or additional shares of stock. This falls anywhere from a week to a month after the ex-dividend date. The delay is needed in order for the company to verify all of the stockholders of record and ensure that dividends are credited properly.

cum dividend

Meaning "with dividend," in reference to the status of a stockholder entitled to receive a dividend in the current quarter.

Examples

It's a date: You bought shares of stock when you saw that the company declared its first dividend payment. For you, that meant it would be valuable to own shares. The following May 10 was ex-dividend date. You sold your shares on May 17. However, on June 5, which was the payment date, you received the dividend even though had sold your shares. The reason: Before ex-dividend date you were the stockholder of record.

Examples

Late for the date: You like the 5 percent dividend on a stock you have been tracking so you bought 100 shares on August 16. On payment date of September 13, you did not get the dividend you expected. When you looked into the matter, you realized that ex-dividend date was August 10, and on that date you did not own shares. So you did not earn the dividend. These dates are summarized on the calendar in Figure 6.2.

OCTOBER

Sunday	Monday	Tuesday	Wednesday	Thursday	Friday	Saturday
	1 DD	2	3	4	5	6
7	8	9	10	11	12	13
14	15	16	17	18	19	20
21	22 EX	23	24 RD	25	26	27
28	29	30	31			

■ Non-trading day

DD Declaration date

EX Ex-dividend date

RD Record date

PD Payment date

NOVEMBER

Sunday	Monday	Tuesday	Wednesday	Thursday	Friday	Saturday
				1	2	3
4	5	6	7	8	9	10
11	12	13	14	15	16	17
18	19	20	21	22	23	24
25	26 PD	27	28	29	30	

Figure 6.2
Calendar of Dividend Dates

PICKING STOCKS FOR DIVIDENDS

Every investor has to struggle with the question of how to pick stocks. Do you favor conservative, well-managed companies that have been around for a long time? Do you apply a long-term trend on a few basic fundamental indicators? What are the criteria for picking stocks most likely to perform at the market or even to outperform?

The problem goes back to the question of risk. Price volatility means more rapid movement, but that can occur in either direction. So the more likely a company's stock is to rise, the greater the associated risk that it will fall.

You may pick stocks based on a few sound fundamental indicators like those explained in Chapter 5; or rely on technical trends (see Chapter 12). In either case, you are likely to come down to a very short list of companies that meet all of your criteria. At this point, how do you decide?

Key Point

The dividend yield may be a tie-breaker in trying to decide between two companies whose fundamental strength is equal. The higher dividend yield means higher income from investing in that stock.

dividend achievers

Companies that have declared and paid dividends without missing a payment for 10 years or more, and that have increased the dividend per share every year.

That is where dividend yield comes into the picture. Assuming all other criteria are equal, pick the stock yielding the best dividend. This makes sense, assuming that the yield is consistent and strong. In fact, one of your selection methods may be to focus on *dividend achievers*, defined as companies that have consistently paid dividends over at least 10 years and have increased the dividend per share every year. The idea, founded by Mergent, Inc., in 1979, has become very popular among investors. Several exchange-traded funds (ETFs) are set up to track dividend achievers, including two PowerShares funds (PFM and PEY) and a Vanguard fund (VIG) that tracks Mergent's dividend achievers stocks.

Why focus on dividend achievers? As a general rule, the companies meeting this 10-year requirement are exceptionally well-managed and consistent in many fundamental ways. Their prices also have trended upward for the most part. In order for a company to increase its dividend every year, it has to earn profits and manage its working capital effectively. Dividends can be paid out only if enough cash income is generated to make the payments every quarter.

Valuable Resource
You can find out about the dividend achievers program and how the selection is made at the Mergent website: **www.mergent.com/productsServices-print-dividendArchivers.html**.

An ETF that tracks dividend achievers might also be appealing to you. Several ETFs are focused on this special attribute of a company. See a list of ETFs specializing in this manner at **www.etftrends.com/2010/03/dividend-etfs-aristocrats-vs-achievers/**.

A second method for picking stocks is to focus on what are called the *dogs of the Dow*. This is a stock-picking strategy isolating the stocks in the Dow Jones Industrial Average (the Dow) that currently pay the highest dividend yield. The 10 highest-yielding stocks in the 30 companies are included. The theory is that stocks with the largest yields have probably been beaten down in price and are most likely to rebound. In addition, by investing in the dogs, you get the highest yields.

Remember, however, that one reason for high dividends is a price decline. And although this might be a swing likely to reverse in the near future, it also could be the start of a longer-term decline in price. Over the past few years, many companies (such as General Motors, Eastman Kodak, or Citicorp, for example) experienced big drops in prices, not just as part of a swing, but as part of a more disastrous fall in value. So the dogs of the Dow strategy is simple and easily applied, but it could be risky.

A final strategy worth mentioning is a timing strategy. In this idea, you buy stocks before the ex-dividend date with the intention of selling them right after. This entitles you to the dividend, while you churn capital in and out of stocks to get dividends every month instead of every quarter.

The idea seems flawless at first glance. But again, it is risky. You have to expect a stock's price to drop on ex-dividend date or soon after, to reflect the obligation to pay out dividends. So you could end up earning a dividend but losing it back in depreciated share value. This problem can be overcome in some cases by accompanying stock purchase with the use of options; but in order to make this work, you need to understand how options work and what risks are involved.

Key Point

Buying shares right before ex-dividend date seems logical at first glance. But the dividends you earn are likely to be offset by a decline in the stocks' value on the same day.

For most investors, finding high-quality value companies (well-managed, with a history of steady growth in revenues, earnings, and dividends) is one wise approach. Reinvesting dividends creates a compounding effect that is small in a single year but accelerates over many years.

Even so, for many people, picking the best stock and timing the decision is very difficult. The need to diversify even with a limited capital pool makes individual stock investing higher risk than many people are comfortable with based on risk tolerance standards.

So one alternative worth looking at is buying into automatic diversification through one of several mutual fund choices. The next chapter explains the many kinds of mutual funds, the fees involved, and the investment objectives funds offer.

TO BE CONTINUED...

7

ALTERNATIVES: STOCKS OR MUTUAL FUNDS

For some investors, buying carefully picked stocks in well-managed, successful companies is a smart choice. As value investors, this route assumes that the important groundwork is done through analysis and comparison, and that the time is taken to understand not only the profit potential, but also the risk.

Buying stocks directly is not the only way to invest; however, many people who start out working with others or focusing on mutual funds eventually learn enough about the market that they feel comfortable buying stocks directly. It's a matter of personal choice and comfort, not to mention experience. A mutual fund is a conduit investment, meaning the fund's management handles portfolio decisions for its investors and passes through all profits in the form of dividends, interest, and capital gains. The fund acts as a conduit between the components of the portfolio and each investor.

INVESTMENT CLUBS

Some novice investors will eventually get to the point where they will feel safe buying stocks directly. However, that prospect can be daunting as well. For these individuals, some alternatives are available and can help not only to ease the apprehension, but also provide an education along the way. An investment club is a good place to start.

There are many ways to join or form an investment club. One of the best is to join the National Association of Investors Corporation, which supports over 8,600 investment clubs and has more than 90,000 individual members.

Valuable Resource
The NAIC (**www.betterinvesting.org**) is an association of individuals belonging to investment clubs. They provide publications, forms, and advice from experts and fellow members.

Most clubs hold monthly meetings and members agree to deposit a fixed amount every month to pool together. At the meeting, the research shared by members is explained and discussed, and when appropriate the members decide which stocks to buy. Most clubs have about 15 members. Once club size moves above 20 or 25, it becomes difficult to keep the organization working smoothly and agreeing on a course of action.

Examples

Funds Acting like Stocks: You have decided to buy shares of a closed-end mutual fund. Unlike the more common open-end variety, you have to buy shares on the open market, and at the current price. You discover that due to one fund's excellent performance, the current price per share is higher than the net asset value. You buy shares because you believe that the attribute of being closed makes this more valuable than an open-ended fund. Additionally, limits on the total assets ensure greater portfolio flexibility, and that is very appealing.

Key Point

Anyone apprehensive about picking stocks on their own will benefit by looking into investment clubs as a way to pool resources and capital.

A wise starting point is to agree among members and potential members on an investing philosophy and how research is to be shared. Most NAIC members subscribe to a conservative theory and rely almost exclusively on fundamental analysis of stocks to develop a list of investment candidates. If a club is to take greater risks or speculate in the market, all members should agree; otherwise this strategy will not be appropriate, especially for those new to investing.

Key Point

Investment clubs work only if all members agree on the investing objective and appropriate risk level.

Investment clubs meet regularly every month, which is a good idea because it allows members to set aside the same time every month to attend meetings, and also lets people know how much time they have to complete their research before the next meeting date. The meeting is often held in a member's home, a local library, a church hall, or a coffee shop. The agenda for each meeting should be structured well, and should include updates on the portfolio's performance, research presentations by members, a talk by a guest speaker if available, and decisions about whether to invest in any additional stocks. The complete meeting should not exceed two hours at the most.

Since investment clubs pool members' money, they need to be set up with a formal organization and contract. NAIC helps decide which organizational form to use for an investment club. In addition, club members might want to pick a broker by referral and vote; or they might decide to be completely self-directed and use one of the many online discount brokerages.

Clubs generally need some form of organizational leadership as well. Clubs don't want to become overly formal, but electing officers and leaders of meetings just makes sense. At the very least, investment clubs need to elect a president or presiding partner, an assistant, a treasurer or financial manager, and a secretary or recorder.

Investment clubs can provide a good starting point for you. The shared research and acquired experience of 15 people is a powerful force, and it helps many people to gain knowledge and experience efficiently and profitably. For many others, mutual funds have been a popular choice for many decades.

open-end fund

A type of mutual fund that does not place limits on its number of subscribers or assets it manages.

closed-end fund

A mutual fund with a maximum number of shares outstanding, which trades over a stock exchange rather than directly between fund management and investors. Market value of shares rises or falls based on demand and performance rather than on the market value of the portfolio.

TYPES OF MUTUAL FUNDS

The mutual fund industry is huge. There are thousands of choices for investors, and many different types of funds. These types are defined by investment objective as well as by the cost to invest. Objectives include growth or income, conservative versus speculative, and even type of investment. Some funds specialize in regions or countries, others in specific sectors or types of companies. Any theme you can imagine has probably been set up and organized in some type of mutual fund.

The basic type of mutual fund is an *open-end fund*, meaning that the fund will accept as many investors and as much money as it can raise, without limitation. So a successful fund is likely to grow over time as a growing number of new people open accounts and send in their dollars. This is the most common and popular type of mutual fund.

Compared to the open-end fund, the *closed-end fund* does place restrictions on the number of shares outstanding. While the open-end fund allows investors to buy and then redeem shares directly with the fund management, a closed-end fund is more like a stock. Shares are traded over a stock exchange and could actually grow in value above the true asset value of the portfolio, if demand for those shares is strong enough based on the fund's performance

There are few closed-end funds available today, and for every closed-end fund there are more than 13 open-end funds on the market. The newest type of mutual fund is the exchange-traded fund (ETF), which also trades on stock exchanges and contains a pre-identified *basket of stocks* in its portfolio. In 1995, there were only two ETFs; by the end of 2008, there were more than 700 and the number expands rapidly every year.

A final broad classification in the mutual fund group is called a *unit investment trust (UIT)*. This is a type of fund that buys bonds and other income-generating securities, pools them together and then sells shares to investors. A UIT is not actively managed like a traditional mutual fund, because the portfolio of income securities is purchased in advance. Payments are made for capital gains, dividends, and interest as these are earned.

basket of stocks

The pre-identified, fixed portfolio in the exchange-traded fund (ETF).

unit investment trust (UIT)

A fund that purchases income-generating securities (bonds and stocks) and creates a trust in which shares are sold to investors. Periodic payments are made for interest, dividends, and capital gains earned throughout the life of the UIT.

Key Point

The ETF as an alternative to the traditional mutual fund makes sense; it is easily traded, management fees are minimal, and the portfolio is picked in advance.

Valuable Resource

For more statistics and information about mutual funds, check the Investment Company Institute website at **www.ici.org**, and to see the complete annual Fact Book ICU publishes, go to **www.icifactbook.org**.

MUTUAL FUND FEES

One of the biggest problems with picking a mutual fund is the variety and number of fees that might or might not be involved. The success of mutual fund investing has made it especially complex, and making valid comparisons is difficult. Some fees are hidden; some apply when you sell rather than when you buy; and some are given different names from one fund to another.

sales load

A commission deducted from investments in mutual funds and paid to the salesperson.

load funds

Mutual funds that deduct a sales commission from all investments made, to be paid to a salesperson who recommends the investment.

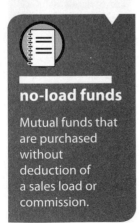

no-load funds

Mutual funds that are purchased without deduction of a sales load or commission.

> **Key Point**
> Making like-kind comparisons among mutual funds is so difficult because the many different fees vary and are given different names.

The range of fees includes the *sales load*. This fee should apply only when you buy mutual fund shares through a broker or financial planner. As the name says, this is a sales commission paid to the salesperson who recommends a fund to you. A common fee is 8.5 percent, meaning that the minute you invest $100, the load of $8.50 is deducted and given to the salesperson.

The fee comes off the top, meaning that only $91.50 of your $100 goes into the investment. The group of funds known as *load funds* are those that deduct this commission. However, even if you purchase shares directly and without assistance from a financial planner, you might have this sales load deducted. Over history, there has been no trend of load funds outperforming the commission-free funds you can buy on your own, known as *no-load funds*.

A justification for paying a sales load would be that a financial planner has researched and compared all available funds and knows that the fund he or she is recommending is most likely to perform well in the market. This also assumes that the broker or planner has examined the portfolio and investment experience of management and has seen a clear distinction of one fund's performance over another. These assumptions are not necessarily true. The problem comes down to that commission. A salesperson who is compensated by commission is not going to recommend a no-load fund even if it is likely to outperform a comparable load fund. In addition, you should not assume that the research and comparison of investment value has even been performed before a recommendation is made.

Key Point

If a financial expert is promoting a load fund as your best choice, ask for proof based on recent performance. Paying a sales commission does not ensure that you will be investing in a better choice.

The load is also called a *front-end sales load* because the commission is deducted right off the top before your capital is invested in shares of the mutual fund. Recognizing how disadvantageous this is, some mutual funds have devised what is called a *back-end sales load*. This is a fee deducted when you redeem shares, so that the sales commission comes out of your accumulated investment plus earnings, rather than being taken before the investment is even made.

The back-end load may not be charged at all. In some very popular arrangements, the back-end load is actually called a *contingent deferred sales load (CDSL)*. This is charged only if you redeem shares within a specified period of time. If you hold shares beyond that deadline, the fee will not be assessed. The contingent load may be reduced over a period of years, eventually falling to zero for extended holding periods.

A mutual fund calling itself a no-load fund will not deduct a sales load, but many do assess other fees given a broad array of names. These include purchase fees, redemption fees, exchange fees, or account fees. None of these are considered sales loads as long as they do not exceed ¼ percent of the current value of an account. So a fund describing itself as no-load might charge fees under a different name.

front-end sales load

An alternative name for the load, so called because a sales commission is deducted from an investment before funds are used to buy mutual fund shares.

back-end sales load

A variation of sales commission in a mutual fund, in which the commission is deducted when shares are redeemed, rather than when investments are made.

contingent deferred sales load (CDSL)

A back-end load, or sales commission assessed by mutual funds only if shares are redeemed before a specified number of years.

redemption fee

A charge assessed by a mutual fund at the time that shares are redeemed, not to exceed 2 percent of the redemption value.

 Key Point
A fund called no-load is not always the cheapest to buy; a variety of fees and charges might apply.

A *redemption fee* differs from a back-end sales load in the sense that it is not paid to a salesperson, but is described as covering the cost the fund has to absorb when it redeems your shares. Redemption fees are limited to 2 percent or less of the value of redeemed shares.

All mutual funds charge some fees. These include the *management fee*, which is compensation for the professionals who research companies and make buy and sell decisions in the portfolio. The real test of a fund's value—whether load or no-load—is how effectively management makes its decisions and selects stocks or bonds to include in the portfolio.

Funds also assess numerous other fees, with descriptions like custodial expenses, legal and accounting expenses, or administrative expenses.

Finally, an important kind of fee that might be charged by either a load or no-load fund is called a *12b-1 fee*. Also called a distribution or service fee, this fee gets its name from the SEC rule permitting it (Rule 12b-1).

This rule allows a fund to charge a fee for advertising and marketing of the fund, including printing and mailing a fund *prospectus* to new potential investors.

So a 12b-1 fee is charged to current investors to raise money to attract new investors. This fee cannot be greater than ¾ of 1 percent of the fund's average net assets during the past year. Some funds mask fees intended for promotional activities by calling them *shareholder service fees*, which pay compensation to individuals who respond to shareholder inquiries or questions. This fee may be assessed separately or as part of a 12b-1 fee. If it is set aside separately, it cannot exceed ¼ of a percent of the fund's asset value.

management fee

The fee charged by a mutual fund to compensate its professional managers.

Key Point

The 12b-1 fee is charged to current investors to raise cash to market the fund to *new* investors.

The fee structure of mutual funds is confusing and often misleading, making side-by-side comparisons very difficult. With this in mind, you need to ensure that your comparisons between funds make true and accurate cost analyses as part of the effort.

prospectus

A disclosure document explaining the nature and risks of securities, including management and their compensation, investment objectives, and costs involved in buying shares.

Valuable Resource

You can compare fees, performance, and other facts about mutual funds by using a fund analyzer provided free of charge by the Financial Industry Regulatory Authority (FINRA). To use the analyzer, go to **http://apps.finra.org/fundanalyzer/1/fa/aspx**. A second cost calculator, also free, is available at the Securities and Exchange Commission (SEC) website. Go to **www.sec.gov/investor/tools/mfcc/holding-period.htm**.

CLASSIFICATION BY FEATURES

There are two additional considerations in the selection of funds. First is how fund shares are valued, and second is to understand the distinction between different kinds of mutual funds.

You will find daily listings for *net asset value (NAV)*. This is the ending day value of the fund's entire portfolio, divided by shares outstanding.

NAV is always calculated as of the day's closing prices. An ETF or closed-end fund, in comparison, changes in value throughout the trading day just like shares of stock that are publicly listed. This is most commonly used to track mutual fund performance. As NAV rises, it indicates positive results. And as it falls, it means negative outcome.

shareholder service fees

A mutual fund's charge for expenses of responding to client inquiries, either as part of a 12b-1 fee or separately from it.

net asset value (NAV)

The day's ending value of a mutual fund, computed by adding the total asset value of the fund (minus any liabilities) and dividing the net total by the number of shares outstanding.

Key Point
NAV does not give you the best picture of relative value, because all current earnings are distributed in cash or reinvested to buy new shares; total annual return is a more reliable comparative measurement of fund performance.

However, NAV is not necessarily the best method for judging a fund's performance. Because a fund pays all of its capital gains, dividends, and interest to shareholders, different levels of current income will not be reflected in the reported NAV price. A more accurate measure is the fund's annual total return.

Performance is going to depend on the type of fund and how that classification performs in today's market. Of course, performance also varies based on management's selection of a portfolio and timing for its entry and exit decisions. There are nine major categories. These are:

1. *Equity funds* are the best-known ones. These invest in stocks. Because mutual funds are considered institutional investors, they trade in large blocks of stock compared to the relatively few shares traded by individuals, or retail investors.

2. *Fixed-income funds* (or *income funds*) specialize in either bonds generating interest income, or stocks with exceptionally high dividends. These are both forms of income. Capital gains are also earned in these funds from selling stock above purchase price, or from redeeming bonds at face value when they were purchased at a discount.

3. *Balanced funds* combine potential growth from equity investments with potential income from dividends and interest.

4. *Specialty funds* are designed to pursue companies with specific features, in addition to defining themselves as equity, fixed-income, or balanced funds. An example is the green fund, which includes only green technology companies in their portfolio. A global fund is another specialty fund that seeks positions in a wide selection of international companies.

5. *Money market funds* invest only in instruments in the money market, which are interest-yielding and will not offer growth potential. These include certificates of deposit, U.S. Treasury bills, bankers' acceptances, and commercial paper.

6. *Hedge funds* are not set up or regulated like any others in the fund universe. They are usually private partnerships that accept a limited number of investors and require a large deposit to participate. They use leverage through derivatives and other advanced techniques to create high returns (or high losses).

7. *Capitalization-based funds* specialize in companies of a specific market cap size. So there are large-cap, mid-cap, and small-cap funds suited for investors who believe the best returns will be found in one of those categories.

8. *Index funds* do not buy stocks specifically, but invest in the broader market by tracking performance in an index like the S&P 500, the Dow Jones Industrial Average (DJIA), or other indexes that define and track market performance.

9. *Tax-free bond funds* are similar to fixed-income funds in the sense that they take positions in bonds. However, this group buys only those bonds that are exempt from income tax. To determine whether such a fund is appropriate, investors should compare the after-tax return from the fixed-income fund to the tax-free return in this type of fund.

OTHER CONDUIT INVESTMENTS

In addition to mutual funds, there are many other ways to pool investments with others and within an organized structure. A mortgage pool is a mutual fund-like company that specializes in taking shares of a collection of mortgages. These mortgage-backed securities are offered by lending institutions sponsored or guaranteed by the U.S. government.

equity funds

Mutual funds that create a portfolio from investments in stocks (equities) of listed companies.

Key Point

The widespread failure of mortgage pool–based investments in 2007 to 2009 proves that excessive risk invariably causes a strategy to fail.

fixed-income funds

Mutual funds that purchase bonds to generate interest income or stocks to yield higher-than-average dividends.

secondary market

The government-sponsored market for purchasing of mortgage contracts from lenders, organizing them into larger mortgage pools, and selling shares to investors.

real estate investment trust (REIT)

A real estate investment conduit that trades on public exchanges like shares of stock.

These organizations include the Government National Mortgage Association (GNMA), also known as Ginnie Mae; the Federal National Mortgage Association (FNMA), or Fannie Mae, which also sells REMICs; and the Federal Home Loan Mortgage Corporation (FHLMC), or Freddie Mac. All of these market a mortgage-pool product called the *real estate mortgage investment conduit (REMIC)*.

These mortgage pools have become controversial in recent years, due to excessive marketing and lax credit standards among participating lenders. Collectively, these organizations created a *secondary market* for real estate lending. Local institutions underwrote loans and then sold those loans to one of the big national groups, which then placed the mortgage into a pool with thousands of other loans and sold shares to investors. At least to some extent, excessive secondary market activity is what led to the housing bubble and crash of 2007 to 2009.

Valuable Resource

To learn more about the secondary market for real estate and mortgage pools, check the websites for each of the three major organizations:

1. Ginnie Mae, **www.ginniemae.gov**
2. Fannie Mae, **www.fanniemae.com**
3. Freddie Mac, **www.freddiemac.com**

Another way to own real estate but have it act like stock is through the *real estate investment trust (REIT)*. This is a pooled investment that combines the money of thousands of investors to buy, construct, or develop real estate properties. REIT shares trade on public exchanges just like stocks, making them very liquid.

There are many types of conduits that specialize in all markets: stocks (equity), debt, and real estate. The right one depends on your own risk tolerance and personal investment goals.

Key Point

The REIT is a good way to invest in real estate but maintain liquidity and diversification.

Valuable Resource
Check the complete list of REITs available for public trading, including descriptions and links, at **www.propsolve.com/list_of_reits.html**.

VARIABLE ANNUITIES

A final type of pooled investment is the *variable annuity*. This is similar in many ways to mutual funds, but with some equally important differences as well.

Variable annuities include either a lump-sum investment or periodic investments. An annuity, or series of payments, is guaranteed years later, but the amount varies based not only on how much is deposited, but also on how the portfolio performs.

Key Point
Variable annuities are similar to mutual funds in many ways, but they are insurance products and involve many costs and fees.

Because this is an insurance product and not like other investments, when you buy into a variable annuity, you are not an investor, but an annuitant. The future date when payments will begin is established in advance and is usually a specific age or retirement date. Within the variable annuity you are given a range of choices about where your money will be placed. These include a range of mutual funds, including splitting your money within one mutual fund company, but among a *family of funds* it offers.

variable annuity

A product similar to a mutual fund, which combines investment dollars from many individuals to create a portfolio. The issuing company agrees to make a series of payments in future years based on the value of contributed capital and performance of the securities in the portfolio.

Advantages that variable annuities offer over mutual funds include tax-deferred growth, a death benefit that goes to your beneficiaries and is equal to account value or a guaranteed minimum, and options for how you receive payments later (including a stream of payments for a guaranteed number of years, or guaranteed lifetime income, for example).

Disadvantages include a surrender fee if you withdraw funds early; expense fees that may be greater than comparable fees in mutual funds; and the overall complexity of the variable annuity contract when compared to buying shares in a mutual fund. Because most fees are not charged up front, variable annuities look like no-load funds. But fees are charged during the ownership period in the form of back-end penalties for withdrawal.

 Key Point

The best way to select any pooled investment is by ensuring that it matches your investment objectives, and that you completely understand what fees, risks, and requirements are involved.

Pooled investments—whether organized personally through an investment club, or more formally through a mutual fund, real estate pool, or variable annuity—are popular because they solve a familiar problem for a vast portion of the investing public. They automatically diversify investments, make reinvestment of income easy and automatic, and rely on professional management to make tough portfolio decisions.

The next section of this book discusses an alternative to investing, through various trading techniques. The distinction is made on three levels:

1. *Holding period*: Investment usually means a buy-and-hold strategy over many months or years; trading means moving in and out of positions in very short time spans, days, or even hours.

2. *Risk level*: As a general rule, investors tend to be more conservative and traders more speculative in their market strategies.

3. *Source of information*: Investors are more likely to use fundamental analysis and to rely on financial statements and trends. Traders are more inclined to use technical analysis, study price charts, and time entry and exit based on price trends.

The many strategies used by traders are explained next, beginning with an analysis of trading risks.

family of funds

A group of funds offered by one mutual fund company but with different investment objectives.

TO BE CONTINUED...

PART **2** TRADING

8 THE NATURE OF STOCK TRADING

While an investor tends to buy and hold stocks based on financial indicators and trends, traders focus on price. This might seem like a much different approach to the market, but in fact investing and trading are tied together in many ways.

The fundamental strength or weakness exhibited in financial trends directly affects price strength or weakness. By the same argument, a stock's popularity affects how investors view a company and its fundamentals. For example, if a company's revenue and earnings have been volatile and unpredictable over many years, the conservative investor will be less likely to invest in that stock. The trader may be equally concerned because unpredictability is going to be reflected both in financial and price trends.

Key Point

Investors tend to rely on consistency in trends, meaning low fundamental volatility. This affects traders as well, even when focusing on short-term price movement.

Compare two companies, one with very steady and stable growth and the other with a lot of volatility in both revenues and net profits. Walmart (WMT) exhibited 10 years of very consistent growth as shown in Figure 8.1.

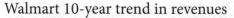

Walmart 10-year trend in revenues

Walmart 10-year trend in net profits

Figure 8.1 Walmart 10-Year Trends

Source: S&P Stock Reports.

This is precisely what fundamental investors want to see, a reliably consistent long-term curve in basic indicators such as revenues and net profits. But not every company will be able to report the same strong long-term trends. For example, Sears Holding (SHLD) reported very volatile revenues and earnings, as shown in Figure 8.2.

Figure 8.2 Sears Holding 10-Year Trends
Source: S&P Stock Reports.

In this case, it is impossible to tell where revenues and profits are likely to go next. Recent years show considerable weakness and Sears announced by 2012 that it was closing many of its Sears and K-Mart stores, the consequence of weakness in its year-to-year numbers.

The fundamental trends of these two companies are vastly different; but how does that translate to the technical side? Figure 8.3 compares the price ranges of both companies over the period.

Key Point

If a company's revenues, earnings, and other indicators are erratic, it is impossible to know what is going to happen next. Fundamental investors prefer certainty, whereas traders tend to thrive on volatility.

Valuable Resource

To generate stock charts for yourself, including tailored criteria and technical tests, go to **www.stockcharts.com**.

Note that the scaling on these two charts is quite different. Walmart is scaled in one-point increments, and Sears Holding is in 10, as shown in Figure 8.3. Walmart, with its less volatile fundamental results, ranged between $42 and $64 over 10 years, a small spread of only 22 points. In comparison, Sears Holding reported a vastly larger price range between $12 and $195, a spread of 183 points. (The Sears Holding record only spans eight years, since the company was not formed until two years into the decade.)

Walmart, Price Range over 10 Years

Sears Holding, Price Range over 10 Years

Figure 8.3 Walmart and Sears Holding Price Range over 10 Years

Source: S&P Stock Reports.

This comparison makes the point that fundamental and technical analysis are directly linked, and actually are different attributes of the same overall volatility and growth trends. Volatility—another name for market risk—normally applies to price, and appropriately so. However, volatility in the financial trends is the same feature, but over a broader scale. The more volatile revenues and profits, for example, the more difficulty investors and traders have in determining where the trend is likely to go next.

Valuable Resource
To calculate a stock's volatility (also called historical volatility) use a free online calculator like the one found at **www.power4xl.com/black_scholes/functions/historical_ volatility.html**.

So traders may continue to focus on price trends, but will also benefit from watching the fundamental indicators and trends. This helps you to identify the best conditions for trading and for analyzing your risks.

FAVORABLE CONDITIONS FOR TRADING STOCKS

Technical analysis is all about price and timing. Most technicians reply on price patterns in charts, combined with volume spikes, *momentum oscillators* (indicators measuring the rate and strength or weakness of trends), and price gaps.

The technician relies on some type of action, movement, reaction or overreaction in price in order to make a move. This move may be to enter a new position or to exit an existing position.

momentum oscillators

Indicators that measure the strength or weakness in price as well as the speed of changes. These include tests of moving averages or the Relative Strength Index (RSI).

Key Point
Those who prefer technical analysis gain information from volatility—and the reversals or changes in momentum that accompany volatility. Without this, the technician cannot be certain of what action, if any, to take.

Valuable Resource
To learn more about momentum oscillators and how to use them, go to stockcharts.com and read the informative article on this topic: **http://stockcharts. com/school/doku.php?id=chart_school:technical_ indicators:introduction_to_tech**.

Relying on patterns seen in charts in both price and volume, and observations of price volatility, technicians employ strategies meant to take advantage of the erratic swings in the market. As a general rule, price tends to overreact to news, events, and even rumors. So an earnings report may come in two cents below expectations and the stock falls four points that day. Technicians recognize that this happens with regularity, and equally reliable is the likelihood that in the following session or two, much of the decline with be reversed. This short-term chaos of price and the tendency to overreact to virtually everything presents opportunities to move in and out of positions.

Examples

The Swinging Times: You are tracking a stock that experiences dramatic prices swings any time news is released or the market moves many points; but you notice that these swings self-correct within one to two sessions. To get a better idea of the differences between momentary price spikes and longer-term trends, you rely on the Relative Strength Index (RSI), recognizing that as long as the index remains within the mid-range, it is likely that the price movement will correct. Only when it moves above or below the mid-range do you get concerned about price movement.

These swings occur frequently. In fact, to the technician, when a stock's price remains in a very narrow range and does not move much, it is not very interesting. To the more fundamental investor, low volatility is reassuring; to the technical trader, price volatility is exciting and immediate, and more to the point, it provides many opportunities.

For example, in Figure 8.4, the three-month chart of the fourth quarter, 2011 for Verizon (VZ) revealed a period of short-term volatility, which some would interpret as uncertainty. Note the *wedge* pattern forming during this period of erratic price movement. The wedge often represents a disruption in an upward trend, after which that trend resumes.

Figure 8.4 Verizon, Example of Short-Term Volatility

Source: Stockcharts.com.

wedge

A price pattern in which the trading range narrows time, often representing a disruption in an uptrend before that trend resumes.

Such volatility does not always occur. In a chart of the same period for Caterpillar (CAT) as shown in Figure 8.5, note the strong uptrend with very little breadth in the price, meaning low volatility. Price then settled into a sideways pattern with low volatility as well. The uptrend ranges only about three points from high to low during the entire period; this is the kind of price movement with low volatility that investors find satisfying, but which traders might find frustrating—if only because overreaction swings are not abundant.

Figure 8.5 Caterpillar, Example of Price Movement with Little Volatility
Source: Stockcharts.com.

Does the tendency to prefer higher volatility mean that technical analysis also presents higher risks in the market? It might and often does, but it is not necessarily a requirement. Traders tend to work with higher risk levels and seek short-term profits from the chaos of price movement. In comparison, investors are more likely to hold stocks for price appreciation based on financial strength and want lower risks.

Key Point

While traders tend to accept higher risks than investors, it is not always true that the two disciplines can be defined strictly along lines of risk. The importance of picking stocks and timing trades applies to both sides.

However, even conservative investors who prefer financial trends as a means for buying and holding stocks can benefit from observations of technical volatility and price movement. For example, investors holding shares for longer-term growth may observe today's price movement as quite erratic. Does this mean they should sell shares? No. Using technical indicators, they can take several actions, including:

1. *Take no action.* The most prudent decision, especially for conservative investors, is to take no action just because share price is volatile in the moment. The reasons for volatility can be many and varied, and as long as these are likely to pass, it is not necessary for investors to be fearful of the short-term price chaos.

2. *Sell and wait out the volatility.* The most risk-conscious investors might decide to sell shares just in case the volatility is a sign of price declines yet to come. This means opportunities could be lost, especially if the volatility goes away or prices move dramatically upward. However, some investors will not be willing to wait and see or to examine circumstances to try and identify the causes of the change in price patterns.

3. *Exploit the volatility in other ways.* Investors using both fundamental and technical indicators may be willing to take advantage of short-term volatility in one of several ways. These include buying more shares, selling off some part of holdings to take profits, or using options to protect against downward movement and exploit upward movement taking place short-term.

4. *Reevaluate the fundamental assumptions.* When volatility is not expected, it could reveal a change in the financial condition of a company. For example, if earnings are disappointingly low and the company lowers its *guidance* for coming quarters, this may lead to a price decline over coming weeks and may be foreshadowed by unusually high volatility right away. In this case, investors may be wise to sell shares and move money to companies with stronger results and forecasts.

So favorable conditions for trading rely on whether you consider yourself conservative or not. If a situation seems high-risk, the more conservative (and likely fundamentally inclined) investor will shy away. However, the same condition may be quite attractive to the trader, or even to investors willing to live with higher than average risks.

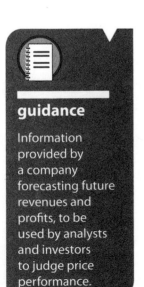

guidance

Information provided by a company forecasting future revenues and profits, to be used by analysts and investors to judge price performance.

RELATIONSHIPS BETWEEN TECHNICAL AND FUNDAMENTAL VALUE

The relationship between fundamental and technical indicators is clear; as a trader, you have the opportunity to improve your own analysis by using both. The combined use of these two sources of information is vital in several ways:

1. *Risk reduction.* The overall risk of investing or trading often is recognized only after losses have occurred. This is a basic flaw with fundamental analysis; by the time the most recent financial statements have been published, known causes for decline in stock prices have taken effect. Fundamental analysts study long-term trends, but the reversal signals occur in the moment. By watching both fundamental trends and current price activity, traders are more in tune with the entire picture.

Key Point

Traders have an advantage because information is available immediately. A fundamental analyst may be weeks or even months behind by the time reports are published.

2. *Improved reliability of selections.* Fundamental investors pick stocks based on financial strength and performance, whereas the trader is likely to rely exclusively on technical indicators. By using both, the selection of companies as long-term, or value investments, is improved: By also monitoring technical trends, notably changes in volatility, those same investments may be judged from different perspectives of value.

3. *Better fundamental choices based on volatility levels.* The volatility in short-term price movement may signal changes well before they are observed in fundamental indicators. This is because long-term trends appear at quarter-end and fiscal year-end reports, which may not be available until two to three months after the cut-off dates. Observing the technical indicators provides early warning signals or opportunity flags even to fundamental investors. This partially overcomes the problem of delayed information chronically suffered by fundamental investors.

4. *Identification of bargain-priced stocks.* Even the most conservative fundamental investor relies on the precepts of value investing, whose most important rule is to buy stock in well-managed, highly competitive companies, at a bargain price. This makes it necessary for fundamental investors to track price while being aware of what constitutes a bargain price. So based on fundamental principles, the value investing requisite relates to the technical attribute of current price.

5. *Improved knowledge for selling stocks.* Fundamental investors must know when to buy stock, but equally important they also need to know when or if to sell. Even the strongest company will not remain a leader in its sector forever. Consider the cases of General Motors or Eastman Kodak as examples. Both of these were once considered the safest blue chip companies and leaders in their industries. But the fundamentals indicators began to deteriorate and price trends accompanied the decline in overall financial strength.

Key Point

Using technical trends to sell stock is just as important as using them to decide when to buy. Profits consist of timing on both sides of the transaction.

The fundamental and technical indicators are quite different, but both are most effective when used together to analyze a company's strength and to determine when to buy or sell shares. The starting point for deciding how to trade should be based on the principle of using both disciplines. From there, identification of the many kinds of trading risks you face is the essential step in this process. The next chapter explains.

THE ADVENTURES OF STOCK·MAN

ON A DARK, DRIZZLY EVENING, *STOCK BOY* WORKS *ALONE*, STOCKING SHELVES AS THE *GRAVEYARD SHIFT* MOVES SLOWLY FORWARD.

SHHH!

WHEN WE ARE HERE, I'M STOCK *BOY* AND YOU'RE STOCK *GIRL*.

SORRY, I DIDN'T MEAN TO BLOW THE *COVER*.

SO YOU'RE WORKING TONIGHT, TOO?

YES, I'M OVER IN THE CHIPS AND BEER AISLE. *BORING.*

YAWN

BETTER THAN CANNED GOODS.

BUT *STOCKING* IS A LOT LIKE *TRADING STOCKS* WHEN YOU THINK ABOUT IT.

SOME ARE MORE BORING THAN OTHERS.

SOUTH SIDE MARKET

THAT SOUNDS VERY *PROFOUND,* STOCK BOY, BUT I'M NOT SURE WHAT YOU *MEAN.*

TO BE CONTINUED...

9 TRADING RISKS

The first section of this book examined the range of techniques known as fundamental analysis, or the selection of companies based on financial strength and performance. In fundamental analysis, you examine the trends a company has reported to pick a logical and reliable investment.

In this section, the alternative—*technical analysis*—is described. Fundamental analysis relies on the most recent history of financial statements and the trends these reveal to pick companies. The technician analyzes price patterns and signs to pick a stock. These two approaches—picking a company based on history or picking a stock based on price patterns—are quite different. However, both fundamental and technical indicators can be used together.

technical analysis

The study of price patterns, charts, and trends to time entry into and exit out of positions in stock, compared to fundamental analysis, which studies trends to pick companies.

Valuable Resource
To expand your knowledge of technical analysis, buy a very informative book by Al Brooks, Trading Price Action Trends: **www.amazon.com/Trading-Price-Action-Trends-Technical/dp/1118066510/ref=pd_sim_b_5**.

exit and entry signals

Indicators consisting of price patterns or changes, which traders use to improve the timing of buy and sell decisions. These signals are meant to improve their chances of accurate timing to increase profits and reduce losses.

confirmation

The use of one indicator to bolster or support the conclusions reached by what a different indicator reveals.

The value of using fundamental and technical indicators together is that this provides you with twice the information. Both sources are worth studying, and neither is exclusively right or wrong for everyone.

Traders are understandably concerned with improving the timing of their trades. So they seek *entry and exit signals* in order to improve their timing. These involve a wide range of indicators that work together or, of equal value, contradict one another. Contradictory indicators should warn a trader away from making a decision merely because there is no clear or strong signal. Traders need reliable and consistent signs.

When you find a company that appears strong in all of the fundamental tests, the technical indicators can be used as *confirmation*, an independent and separate method for verifying the strength of a company as well as assuring yourself that your timing is good. The same confirmation action can work in the opposite direction, with fundamental strength confirming the strength of a stock and timing that technical tests reveal.

Valuable Resource
An informative article on the topic of confirmation can be read on minyanville.com, which is a great site for a range of financial, investing, and trading information. The confirmation article is at **www.minyanville.com/ businessmarkets/articles/stock-market-confirmation- percentage-confirmation-time/1/14/2011/id/32204**.

Chapter 2 examined a series of risks from a fundamental perspective. The following sections take another look at the risk issue, but from a technical point of view.

Key Point
Technical indicators are not only separate methods for timing entry and exit, but are also valuable as confirming signals for fundamentally based investment decisions.

bull markets

Markets
characterized by
generally rising
prices of stocks
over a period of
months or years.

MARKET RISK AND VOLATILITY RISK

The first distinction that has to be made between fundamental and technical analysis is that of risks. An *investor* is most likely to purchase shares of stock as part of a buy-and-hold strategy. This may last years or, for some, only a few months. The selection is based on the company rather than on the price trend in the stock. In comparison, a *trader* is more likely to focus on the price movement and trend in the stock and is much less interested in the fundamental strength of the company.

Valuable Resource
Investopedia.com has an excellent article comparing fundamental and technical analysis: **www.investopedia. com/university/technical/techanalysis2. asp#axzz1t9j5uVaO**.

So investors focus on financial history and traders focus on current price. In summary, that is the most likely distinction between investors and traders; however, you can combine fundamental and technical analysis to round out your opinions of companies and their stocks, time your entry and exit, and diversify your portfolio. This also diversifies your risks, because the types and degrees of risk for investors and traders are not identical. They are quite different.

Key Point
The basic difference between fundamental and technical is in focus, either on historical financial results, or on anticipating price movement.

Market risk is going to be found in all kinds of markets, even those in which price trends are uncertain. Traders are keenly aware of this and tend to develop strategies to maximize profits in *bull markets* (characterized by a trend of rising prices) as well as in *bear markets* (markets where prices are on the decline). Traders believe that by using the right strategies and positioning themselves correctly it is possible to make profits in both kinds of markets. In comparison, those who believe profits are only possible when stock prices are rising (bull markets) by definition have to stay out of the market when they think prices are declining; and that is half the time.

bear markets

Markets of declining price trends over a period of months or years.

speculation

Short-term trading based on price movement in order to maximize profits based on immediate price movements and trends, distinguished from investment, which tends to involve longer-term hold periods.

Valuable Resource
A very thorough and interesting study of bull and bear markets, and their historical cycles, is found at tradingonlinemarkets.com:
www.tradingonlinemarkets.com/Articles/Trend_Following_Strategies/History_of_Stock_Market_Cycles.htm.

Market risk was explained in Chapter 2 and from a fundamental perspective. A fundamental investor (likely as well to be conservative) has to be aware of price volatility even though the selection criteria include mostly or exclusively a range of fundamental indicators. Most fundamental investors seek stocks of companies with exceptional capital and market strength that are likely to rise in value. Traders rely on technical indicators (and are more likely to be drawn toward *speculation* rather than a buy-and-hold strategy), and they understand that price volatility defines risk. So market risk from a fundamental point of view can be clarified and called *volatility risk* for the technical trader. Traders are likely to recognize the potential for profit in either bull or bear markets, and are likely to use a range of different strategies that work in both situations.

Volatility risk is specifically related to the *breadth* of the *trading range*. This is simply the point spread between the most recent high and low price levels at which a stock has traded. Breadth is relative, however. In a $10 stock, a breadth of two points is considerable; in a $100 stock, it is less volatile simply because the stock's price is higher. So breadth defines volatility, and the degree of breadth is the price movement in comparison to the price level of the stock.

The trading range can be thought of as a reflection of supply and demand, just as it works in any other market. In real estate, if houses within one neighborhood usually sell for between $135,000 and $150,000, the trading range of housing is defined between those high and low prices; and the breadth is $15,000. This could also be called a 10 percent breadth, because the price difference between high and low is 10 percent of the high.

Examples

Breadth and Risk: You own two stocks. One has traded in recent months in a very narrow range from a high of $33 per share to a low of $31. The breadth is two points, or 6 percent (points divided by the high price). The second stock has traded in a range between $112 and $118, or six points. Although the point span is greater, the second stock's breadth is only 5 percent (six points divided by the high of $118), thus less volatile. Another way to compare is to imagine the same dollar amount in both, such as 350 shares at $33 ($11,550) versus 100 shares at $115.50 (also $11,550)— these involve exactly the same amount of capital at risk, but different levels of volatility (and remember, volatility is a reflection of market risk).

volatility risk

A technical variation on the broader market risk, involving the degree of exposure traders accept in picking and timing positions in stock.

In the stock market, breadth and trading range are what define volatility risk. The greater the breadth, the greater the risk. For traders, who are most likely to focus on short-term price movement, higher volatility means greater profit potential in a short period of time. It also means greater volatility risk. For most traders, the most realistic approach is to focus on the stocks with moderate volatility, thus accepting moderate volatility risk in exchange for potential profits. If volatility is too high based on a self-defined risk tolerance, the stock is not appropriate. If volatility is too low, then traders will be equally disinterested because in exchange for low risks, profits are also unlikely.

breadth

The span of price movement within the current trading range, representing the number of points of movement over time.

Key Point

The trading range is the entire framework for technical analysis, and for identifying varying levels of price volatility. Virtually all technical indicators rely on observations of price movement in relation to the trading range.

trading range

The distance between recent high and low price levels; the price area in which buyers and sellers currently interact with one another.

support

The lowest price in a stock's trading range, or the low side of the price range at which sellers and buyers are able to agree on price.

resistance

The highest price in a stock's trading range, or the high side of the price range at which both sides can agree to a trade.

Trading range, or the price difference between high and low trading in recent sessions, is the most important technical concept to remember. Without identifying a trading range, you cannot interpret current price movement or identify risk levels.

In technical analysis, two terms are essential, as they frame the trading range and give meaning to the current supply and demand for shares of a particular company. These are *support* and *resistance*. Support is the lowest price in the trading range, or the lowest level at which sellers and buyers can strike an agreement to exchange shares. Resistance is the highest point in the trading range, or the highest level where price agreement is possible under prevailing conditions.

Valuable Resource
Even if you know what support and resistance mean, can you find those price levels on a chart? A great article explaining how to find these levels is provided by www.swing-trade-stocks.com at: **www.swing-trade-stocks.com/support-and-resistance.html**.

The concepts of support and resistance define the majority of technical indicators, and traders rely on the structure provided by the trading range (defined as the price breadth existing between support and resistance) to identify strength or weakness of price movement. Most technical indicators involve price tests of support or resistance. A *breakout* below support or above resistance has significance, whether it represents creation of a revised trading range, or fails and price then retreats back to the established trading range. Many indicators involve failed tests of these borders, often preceding price movement in the opposite direction.

Key Point

The borders of the trading range—support and resistance—are the *lines in the sand* that identify success or failure of all short-term price movement.

The trading range, its breadth, and the action between price and the borders of support and resistance are the entire structure of technical analysis. Trading relies on interpretation of price patterns and, specifically, on how price moves within (or breaks out of) the support and resistance borders.

LEVERAGE RISK

Traders also face the endless challenge of how to make the best use of capital, based on their risk tolerance and willingness to use borrowed funds. Investors have to contend with this as well. Do they limit investments to available cash or use margin accounts to virtually double their potential positions? The more leveraged a position, the more profit potential *and* the greater the risk of loss.

For traders, leverage is just as much of an issue. However, because traders tend (generally) to be willing to assume higher levels of risk than investors, their leverage risk may be greater as well. With more potential for loss, leverage may mean much greater dollar value to loss as well as dollar value to potential profit. This is a reality for traders, and as a consequence many will limit their use of basic tools such as margin accounts simply to keep risks low even in trading strategies demanding greater risk levels. So the overall risk should be part of the equation for traders; greater risks associated with short-term trading can be made even greater by also maximizing the use of a margin account, for example.

breakout

Price movement below support or above resistance, signifying creation of a new trading range or a failed attempt in which prices retreat back to the established trading range.

Key Point

Leverage is a great way to double or triple your profits; it is also an efficient way to expand your losses just as quickly.

To keep this in perspective, ask yourself: Would you max out a homeowners' equity line of credit (HELOC) to free up funds to trade stocks? Most people would reject this as too high-risk and also as an action likely to threaten the security of their home. However, the same people who would deem using home equity too risky might use a margin account to double up their positions in stocks. If the stocks lose market value, the money borrowed in a margin account has to be repaid.

Examples

A Penny Borrowed Is a Penny Earned? You run your portfolio through a margin account. Just buying and selling shares of stock, you are allowed to leverage up to 100 percent (meaning half cash and half margin). But is this wise? You have $20,000 in value and borrow another $20,000 to hold $40,000 in stock. This is great if the value doubles to $80,000, which creates a profit of $60,000 before the interest you pay on the borrowed funds. But what happens if the value drops by one-half, from $40,000 to $20,000? In this outcome, your net value is zero; you own $20,000 on margin, so leverage has wiped out all of your capital.

CHOMP CHOMP

Under the margin rules, you have to maintain 50 percent in cash and securities, meaning you can borrow $20,000 in your margin account and create stock positions of up to $40,000. If the prices of stocks go up 20 percent, the $40,000 placed into shares of stock increases in value to $48,000. The $8,000 profit is great, and is twice what you would have profited using only cash. However, what happens if the positions lose 20 percent? Now the account is valued at only $32,000. Because you have to maintain that 50 percent value in your margin account, you would get a margin call from your broker, and would be required to either come up with another $8,000 or sell some of your holdings. The $8,000 would restore value to $40,000 and satisfy the 50 percent margin requirement. If you do not meet the margin call, your broker then sells $8,000 of your holdings. This reduces your account value to $24,000 and also reduces your margin to $12,000.

Leverage risk for traders based on maximum margin can be described as the risk of losing twice as much in exchange for the potential of gaining twice as much. Before creating maximum margin positions, it is important to understand this risk and to be willing to accept it or, if not, to avoid margin trading altogether.

Key Point
Margin-based investing is simply getting access to the potential for doubling profits—or losses.

Another way that traders use leverage is through the use of *options* in addition to buying and selling shares of stock. Options are intangible contracts to buy or sell lots of 100 shares of stock. They cost only a fraction of what it would cost to trade 100 shares, and that is where options are so attractive and have become popular as a trading and speculative tool.

Options are attractive not only as speculative tools, but also as a means for managing a portfolio. For long-term investors, options can provide insurance for paper profits, or create short-term profits for no added market risk. However, they are complex instruments and are more completely explained in the third section of this book.

For the moment, it is only necessary to understand that options are excellent leverage products. However, they involve specific types of risk. Your brokerage firm will allow you to trade options only once you have established your experience in options trading and knowledge of risks. You also need to maintain a level of account value in order to trade options, which requires a margin account; and brokerage firms require minimum account value before the margin account is available.

Brokerage firms assign trading levels for options trading. Under the lowest level, you are allowed only the most basic of trading techniques. More than any other method of trading, options are complex in terms of the jargon and sheer number of possible strategies. Some are very high-risk and others are quite conservative. Remember, however, that as with all kinds of strategies, knowing the range of risk is the essential first test you need to pass before placing money into the market. This applies to options and other forms of leverage more than with the act of just buying stock.

SHORT POSITION RISK

Traders can take up two general kinds of positions in the market, whether involved with stocks, options, or exchange-traded funds (ETFs). The best known of these two is a *long position*. Under this approach, you buy shares of stock or an ETF (or an option contract). The sequence of events is the well-known buy-hold-sell.

Traders can also take up the opposite approach, the *short position*. Under this approach, you sell shares (or options) as a first step. This exposes you to substantially higher market risks.

For most traders, the long position is better known whether it involves all cash or margin (or other forms of leverage). Traders who use short positions generally take much greater risks. *So short position risk* describes using the initial sale to create profits when the value of the stock falls, or involves the risk of loss if and when the value rises.

Short positions are used in a variety of different ways. Selling stock, a strategy called *short selling*, is a complex and potentially high-risk strategy. Under this approach, your brokerage firm borrows the shares of stock and lends them to you to sell. So you have to pay interest on the borrowed stock while also being exposed to market risk. You hope the price of stock will fall so you can close the position at a profit. If the price rises, the transaction ends up in a loss.

Most people new to trading will be likely to avoid short selling as an acceptable strategy. The risk level and cost of shorting stock are too high for most individuals; and with the use of options, it is possible to play a bear market without needing to go short.

EXTREME REACTION RISK

Imagine mortgaging your house to get all the money you could, selling everything else you own, and converting all your assets into speculating on the price of a single tulip bulb.

As insane as that sounds, it happened in the 17th century, not just to one person but to a spectrum of people from all walks of life. This famous example of a market mania has been called the tulip mania and it had a disastrous outcome. The prices of tulip bulbs exchanged as commodities ran up to unbelievable levels when speculation fever took over and thousands of people wanted to get in on the amazing profits. The rarity of tulip bulbs was the beginning of the problem. A seed may require 5 to 10 years to produce a tulip flower and another 3 to 5 years to work itself into a bulb. Rarity is also defined by specific color markings. In 1635, the commodity trading activity began on tulips still in the ground, and the action was done via promissory notes instead of the exchange of cash. Trading even went beyond this, with sales made for tulips that had not yet been planted. This was called a windhandle (wind trade).

long position

Ownership of shares, accomplished by a buy order and involving the sequence buy-hold-sell.

short position

The sale of shares, accomplished with an opening sell order and involving the sequence sell-hold-buy.

Key Point
As irrational as the tulip mania was, it was not an isolated case of temporary insanity. Trading in all markets is always susceptible to manias of exactly the same kind.

Prices ran up very quickly, within less than one year, and one record-level sale involved the sale of 40 bulbs for 100,000 florin. To put this in perspective, a ton of butter was worth 100 florin at that time. Two years

short selling

The act of borrowing stock and then selling it in the hope that the price will fall. If that occurs, shares can be closed by buying at a lower price. If the stock price rises, it creates a loss because the short position has to be closed (bought) at a higher price. Short sellers also have to pay interest on the shares borrowed to open the short position.

after it began, the bubble reached its peak and very quickly evaporated. Thousands of speculators, mortgaged and leveraged to the hilt, were completely destroyed practically overnight.

This puzzling event took place on a large scale and involved commodity prices running into outrageously high price levels. It relied on a true mania, a form of greed in which those on the outside think they are losing the opportunity to get rich like everyone else. They take risks they cannot really afford and get into the market, and the new demand creates even higher prices.

Valuable Resource

An excellent chapter on the infamous tulip mania is found in *Extraordinary Popular Delusions and the Madness of Crowds* by Charles Mackay. This book can be ordered on Amazon.com at **www.amazon.com/Extraordinary-Popular-Delusions-Madness-Crowds/dp/051788433X**.

There are three issues that define greed buying like this. First, when profits look easy or automatic, logic is abandoned. People will pay anything just to get a position in the market as long as they are sure prices will keep rising. Second, speculators think the upward move will never end. And third, speculators do not set exit levels for themselves, where they will take their profits and get out. Oddly, when asked, speculators express the belief that they will somehow just know when prices are peaking. The truth is that as long as there is someone else willing to pay more, speculation looks like a game impossible to lose. But the day finally arrives when the new speculators run out. The greater fool theory—the belief that there are always plenty of people who will pay more than you did—only works for a while.

Key Point

Greed trumps logic; it also trumps risk awareness and ultimately destroys a speculator's plan to double up and get out.

The same mentality works when markets are falling. Panic is just as irrational as greed, and traders will sell out of positions to avoid bigger losses tomorrow. The result of greed and fear is that traders may buy high and sell low instead of taking the sage advice to buy low and sell high.

The *greed and panic risk*—or *extreme reaction risk*—can be expressed in another way: "Bulls can make money, and bears can make money. Pigs and chickens get slaughtered."

Tulip mania was not just an oddity that happened once 400 years ago. Similar manias have occurred throughout the history of trading in stocks and commodities, even quite recently. Between 1995 and 2000, the dot-com bubble that created the new Internet sector at one time had thousands of companies selling stock, many of which produced no products and offered no services. As many inexperienced first-time entrepreneurs became millionaires overnight based on nothing but a public offering, a growing number of others jumped onto the trend. Today, many of the most successful companies are survivors of the dot-com years, but for every success story there are hundreds of cases of people losing everything, not only in start-up offerings, but also in speculation in the stock of these new companies that have nothing in the way of assets or even products.

greed and panic risk

The risk that buying will occur irrationally when prices are running up too far and too fast, or that selling will occur when prices are falling rapidly.

Key Point

The dot-com fad of recent history was just as illogical as any other mania. Traders invested fortunes in companies with no tangible assets and no product or service. It's no surprise that most of the dot-com companies are no longer around.

extreme reaction risk

The risk that timing of buying or selling decisions will be based on overreaction to market conditions rather than rationally based or based on observed technical signals.

At various times in the history of the United States, investment crazes have occurred in real estate, cotton, railroads, canals, the auto industry, time-share computers, and biotechnology, to name only a few industries. In most of these instances, the few companies that survived produced a product that had a market, but often with too many players. For example, in 1910 there were more than 200 auto manufacturers selling cars in the United States.

TECHNICAL KNOWLEDGE AND EXPERIENCE RISK

In Chapter 2, knowledge and experience risk for fundamental investors was analyzed and explained. This referred to the actual investing background an individual needs to have before being able to realistically understand the stock market and how it works.

Of equal importance is a variation of the same idea, or *technical knowledge and experience risk*. This is quite different than the fundamental risk requiring an understanding of financial statements and trends. On the technical side is the range of price and *volume* trends and measurements of price movement. This includes a lot of formulation and the study of how different moving averages converge or diverge: how subtle shifts in price patterns or *gaps* in between trading sessions change the picture and anticipate what comes next. The name *technical* analysis is accurate because it is very technical and in many instances difficult to grasp.

The need for a keenly developed interpretive skill cannot be emphasized too much. Technical analysis is focused primarily on price trends or, more to the point, on anticipating price direction based on the most recent indicators. Many of these are hard to spot or can be misread; even the best-understood technical signal can also turn out to be a *failed signal*, meaning that an indicated direction simply does not materialize. Technicians attempt to manage or spot failed signals by confirming what appears to be going on or by waiting for a secondary change in the current trend.

The technician who relies on the study of price indicators is also called a *chartist* because he or she studies price charts of selected stocks in the attempt to spot entry and exit signals, and to make a move before the larger market also recognizes what is going on. A chartist who succeeds in the early detection of developing price changes is probably more experienced than the average trader, and knows how to interpret signals as well as spot a potential failed signal.

technical knowledge and experience risk
The risk that a range of technical indicators is difficult to explain without a background in interpreting them and recognizing their significance and effect on price trends.

TECHNICAL RISK AND MARKET CULTURE

Technical analysts are different kinds of people than fundamental analysts. Technicians enjoy the fast-paced action of the moment and are probably more willing to take risks as traders. Fundamentalists take greater comfort in historical trends and the potential for sustained long-term growth, even to the extent of ignoring and completely discounting the chaos of short-term price movement.

Key Point
Investors cannot simply become traders overnight. The risk tolerance is different and each discipline defines different kinds of people, with different philosophies about the markets and how to use them.

The topic of risk is different from a technical point of view as well. Fundamental risk is related specifically to historical financial strength and operating trends. In comparison, *technical risk* is related to price volatility and trends and to related indicators (like volume, for example) that also are derived from trading action.

Technical risk management requires traders to select stocks for trading that match risk tolerance, and that reflect known volatility the trader finds acceptable. This is very focused, because it involves price as a primary indicator (and for some the only indicator). Compared to fundamental risk management, this is a more concentrated form of risk management. Fundamental analysis has to test many factors including profit and loss, capital strength and working capital, dividend trends, competitive stance within a sector, and quality of management. Technicians seek indicators that anticipate changes in price movement of the stock. There is a lot involved in this process, but the focus is narrow.

An observation of fundamental and technical analysis is often summarized as being the difference between hindsight and foresight, investing and trading, low risk and high risk, or conservative and speculative. These generalizations may apply, but not in every instance. An equally important difference is a reflection of market culture itself. There are significant differences in the perspectives of investors and traders that also show up as different attitudes and opinions between fundamental and technical approaches to the market.

Among the many adages about the market, one applies to help make a distinction between the two groups. That is, the *market rewards patience.* Fundamental investors tend to be very patient and methodical in their approach to the market, but technical traders need and want results immediately, perhaps within the trading day.

Some people on the technical side find the fast entry and exit to be exciting and stimulating, and it is. Traders may be classified as occasional players in the market or as high-volume traders. For example, *day trading* is an activity in which trades tend to be entered and exited within a single trading session. So by the end of the day, no open positions remain.

volume
The level of trading in a stock, represented by the number of shares exchanged between buyers and sellers in a specified period of time (a trading day, for example).

gaps
Spaces in trading found between one session's close and the next session's open.

From a regulatory point of view, day trading presents a problem of a different kind of risk. All margin requirements are based on positions at the end of each trading day, so day traders can execute a high level of trades and use leverage to expose themselves and their brokerage firm to risk, but without incurring any margin requirements. For this reason, a requirement was put in place to identify *pattern day traders* and require them to maintain a minimum cash and securities value of $25,000 in their accounts. This individual is defined as anyone who executes trades in the same stock four times or more within five consecutive trading sessions. If orders reach this level, they will be banned if the trader does not have an account with the broker with at least $25,000 in cash or securities.

Valuable Resource
To learn more about the rules governing pattern day traders and margin requirements that apply, go to **www.finra.org/Investors/SmartInvesting/AdvancedInvesting/DayTrading/P005906**.

Day traders do not close positions the same day they are opened specifically to get around margin requirements. Many traders believe that trading trends can be identified and acted upon within very short time periods. In fact, one of the amazing facts observed by traders is that chart and price patterns occur regardless of the time duration being studied.

Most people who are not day traders use daily charts as the default time duration, and technical patterns are observed on a day-to-day basis. This works for non–day traders willing to hold positions open for more than a single trading session. The day trader, however, uses charts based on more frequent changes. With the Internet, it is easy to create instant charts and track live feeds for any listed stock, with increments that track on any

failed signal

A technical signal indicating a price direction about to emerge (most notably a price reversal) that does not materialize or is contradicted in actual price movement.

time period desired. For day traders, five-minute charts provide valuable information about developments in price trends as they evolve.

chartist

A trader who studies price patterns through a series of stock charts, looking for early signs for emerging entry or exit points based on how price and volume behave, and using a range of possible technical indicators to make those decisions.

Key Point

The observed price patterns that are used to signal entry or exit work in all time durations. So whether you use a daily chart or a five-minute chart, you will find the same technical signals.

The five-minute chart patterns that develop are going to exhibit the same price and chart trends as the daily charts do. However, in a daily chart, the trend encompasses an entire day and many interim price patterns do not show up. So the day trader's argument for more frequent increments in charts is that many entry and exit opportunities are lost in the longer-term chart. Of course, this rapid-action charting system is not for every-one. The dedicated day trader is likely to observe hour-by-hour tendencies in price patterns. A lot of study has gone into analyzing how price trends develop throughout the typical trading day. For example, some traders will tell you not to make trading decisions in the day's first hour. Others believe it is a mistake to put in an order during the Wall Street lunch hour. And many believe that the last hour of the day is when most trends make their move.

technical risk

Any risk directly involving price, reflected in price volatility and trends as well as in related indicators such as trading volume.

Key Point

Isolating trading activity to specific times of day adds yet another element of timing to the technical decision. Traders find methods that work for them and provide discipline to make their strategies work.

For anyone inexperienced in trading, the world of day trading is probably too risky. However, the excitement of making decisions by the hour or even by the minute is difficult to match. The more analytical, long-term fundamental approach is comparatively dry and unexciting, even if it may ultimately be more profitable. The truth is that picking high-value stocks and holding them for many months or years is usually profitable, but traders need and want that daily action to make the experience satisfying.

This is the big difference in market culture. The fundamental analyst is likely to be a value investor using a buy-and-hold strategy. The trader, especially the day trader, does not want to own stock for more than the minimum time needed to generate a profit. There are merits and flaws in both systems, without any doubt. It makes the most sense to remain open-minded to both strategies, and even to combine investing and trading in your portfolio.

The next chapter expands on the discussion of trading to examine day trading in more detail, and to compare various trading systems.

day trading

Activity in which positions are entered and exited on the same day, so that no open positions remain by the end of the day.

pattern day trader

Any trader who moves in and out of positions in the same stock four or more times within five consecutive trading sessions, who is required to maintain at least $25,000 in cash and securities in their brokerage account.

JUST OUTSIDE OF TOWN, *STOCK MAN* AND *DEE JONES* VISIT *THE DOWNTREND*, A POPULAR BUT SEEDY AMUSEMENT PARK.

TO BE CONTINUED...

10

TRADING METHODS: DAY AND SWING TRADING

The basic idea of day trading is not difficult to grasp; but there is more to it than just opening and closing positions on the same day. Day traders employ an array of strategies to improve the timing of their entry and exit. Beyond day trading, an expansion of the concept is called *swing trading*. This is a strategic system involving moving in and out of positions in the short-term, usually three to five days and based on recognition of short-term price trends.

Valuable Resource
A worthwhile extended introduction to the basics of swing trading is available at **www.swing-trade-stocks.com/ swing-trading-basics.html**.

Swing traders rely on specific signals for both entry and exit. These signals warn traders about a trend coming to an end and reversing. This process is an expansion of the same principles used by day traders. This chapter expands on a discussion of these two popular trading systems (day trading and swing trading) and a related topic, entry and exit signals and how to use them.

DAY TRADING

opening order

An order placed with a broker to create a position, either long or short.

Day trading is a system involving many technical tools to complete a *round-trip trade* (opening and closing a position) within a single trading session.

A round-trip trade consists of two major steps: opening and then closing a position. Day traders may be involved in long positions, short positions, or combinations of both. In a long position, the series of steps is buy-hold-sell; with a short position, it is the reverse, or sell-hold-buy.

Key Point

Day traders prefer closing positions the same day opened, out of concern for potential price differences between today's close and tomorrow's open.

closing order

An order placed with a broker to close a position, whether it was opened long or short.

In all trades, the first step is the *opening order* and the last step is the *closing order*. These are further distinguished by whether either of these is long or short.

An opening order creates either a buy (long) or a sell (short) action. So the distinction *buy to open/sell to open* is critical to ensuring that orders are placed properly. On the closing side, the distinction is just as important. So *sell to close/buy to close* also instructs the broker to enter the order you intend to place.

Examples

Buy and Sell, Sell and Buy: You are swing trading on a stock that tends to experience short-term price movement of two to three points over a three- to five-day period. At the bottom of the cycle, you begin with a buy to open and at the top you sell to close. Going in the opposite direction, you open a short position at the top of the cycle with a sell to open order and close this at the bottom with a buy to close order.

Day traders have to be familiar with the range of opening and closing orders so that they can avoid placing an order of the wrong type. In addition to mastering order placement terminology, day traders use a series of technical analysis tools, all aimed at helping them to spot trend strength, weakness and reversals, increasing or decreasing momentum, and related volume indicators that help the timing of day trades.

Key Point

Specific price patterns and changes spark swing trading action, based on short-term trends and reversals.

These technical tools can involve a large number of possible indicators. The most popular and most frequently used are:

1. *Charts.* Indicators most often are spotted visually (even indexed or percentage-based indicators are also charted along with price). Of the many kinds of charts available, candlesticks are becoming very popular with traders (see Chapter 11). These charts provide all of the information about price movement in a single formation: opening and closing price, the session's trading range, and the direction of price movement. The shape of candlesticks is also significant and when two or more sticks are analyzed together, specific patterns provide strong clues about a reversal (or continuation) most likely to follow.

buy to open/ sell to open

The type of opening order being placed. A buy to open is used to create a long position, and a sell to open creates a short position

sell to close/ buy to close

The type of closing order being placed. A sell to close is used to close an existing long position, and a buy to close is used to close an existing short position.

convergence/ divergence

In technical analysis, the pattern revealed in two moving averages of different numbers of sessions. As the lines move closer together (converge) or farther apart (diverge) the chartist draws conclusions about the coming price direction.

MACD

A popular technical indicator, meaning moving average convergence/ divergence, the study of trends based on the proximity between price and averages.

2. *Moving average (MA) analysis.* The moving average is among the most important of technical tools, and day traders, more than most technical analysts, rely on MA to spot strength or weakness in the current trend. Among the MA analysis is the use of two MA lines of different duration. For example, watching the movement in a 20-day and a 200-day MA is revealing. The *convergence/divergence* of the MA lines tells the technician when price is likely to reverse directions. A popular variation of this is called *MACD*, which is an acronym for moving average convergence/divergence.

3. *Breadth of trading range analysis.* The trading range is the key to most forms of technical analysis. As this breadth changes, it holds great significance. A broadening breadth reveals growing price volatility; a narrowing breadth tells you two things. First, volatility is declining; second, a reversal from the current trend is quite likely. Chapter 12 includes an explanation of this indicator.

4. *Support- and resistance-based analysis.* Also in Chapter 12 is an explanation of a range of popular technical indicators. The importance of support and resistance is central to all types of technical indicators, and for day traders, these bottom and top trading levels help define risk and potential profits or losses in a short-term strategy.

Day traders use a specific type of strategic timing approach to the market. However, even traders who hold positions open beyond a single trading session most often use the same strategies, but across a less frantic pace. Day traders are specifically associated with some focused trading activities.

Key Point
Variations in day trading include very specific recognition tools; variations in day trading extend beyond single-session open and close activity.

The first style is called *intra-day trading*. A day trader normally opens and closes a position in a single day. The intra-day trader might do the same, or leave a position open until the following session. The usual pattern is for the position to remain open for a period of time between a few minutes and two trading sessions.

Day traders rely on a series of specific entry and exit signals, which are explained later in this chapter. A variation of this approach is *momentum trading*. Under this system, trades are opened and then closed based on a short-term trend (this may last only a matter of minutes, or for the entire trading day). The ideal momentum trade is made at the beginning of the trend and then closed as soon as momentum becomes exhausted or reverses.

Why is momentum trading any different from other approaches to day trading? Momentum traders act specifically on perceived direction of price, and on slowing down of the pace as a reversal and exit signal. A momentum trader is also likely to analyze price trends using extremely short trading increments, such as five-minute charts. In comparison, other day traders are likely to study price patterns and tests of support and resistance to find entry and exit points, and may use charts taking more time, such as one-hour charts, for example. The momentum trader only tracks the direction of price, and other day traders are likely to seek patterns anticipating reversal before it actually occurs.

Key Point

Day and swing traders look for specific price-related patterns. Momentum traders focus on price direction and strength of timing movement.

intra-day trading

A variation of day trading, a strategy in which positions are opened and closed within single trading sessions or, at the most, two consecutive sessions.

momentum trading

A system of day trading based solely on identifying short-term trends and timing entry and exit based on the trend's strength or weakness (momentum).

Another advanced system, one used by momentum traders and other day traders, is to analyze the price action within a single day using multiple time increments. For example, you might combine analysis using 5-, 15-, and 60-minute charts. This achieves multiple views of the same price, based on the fact that some developing reversal points may be hidden in the longer-duration charts but show up in the 5- or 15-minute versions of the same stock. Chartists who watch two or three different charts at the same time understand that price patterns form in all time increments, and they want to be sure they have all of the visual tools possible. A trader using this strategy is also likely to move in and out of positions more frequently than other day traders, based mostly on changes in momentum.

The desire to close positions before the end of the trading day is characteristic of day traders. The criticism that this avoids the legal margin requirements is part of the reason, but not the primary reason that day traders want to move in and out before trading stops. Most day traders do not want to leave their positions open overnight based on the fear that big changes can occur from one session to the next.

In a nicely ordered world, a stock would open close to the price it closed the day before. However, with growing interest in after-hours trading, this is not a certainty. Companies also tend to make earnings and other announcements after the close of trading just to avoid a big impact on the stock's price on the day the announcement is made. So day traders have a point in wanting to be out of open positions; there are just too many variables that can develop. The chance of a big price change between today's close and tomorrow's open is a very real possibility.

Key Point

Yesterday's close and tomorrow's open are not always the same, and often are not even close. This provides a clue about why day traders are concerned about leaving positions open overnight.

Unlike the buy-and-hold investor who thinks in terms of years, traders think in terms of minutes or hours and act accordingly. Over recent years, the average holding period of positions—including both investors and traders—has been on the decline. Figure 10.1 demonstrates the history of average holding periods since 1920.

Figure 10.1 Average Holding Period, Stocks
Source: New York Stock Exchange (NYSE) data.

The trend demonstrated that between 1945 and 1980, the buy-and-hold philosophy reigned within the stock market, and then declined rapidly. Today, trading has replaced a lot of the traditional strategies that value investing supports—even in spite of the successful track record of the buy-and-hold approach.

The causes of these changes, notably after 1975, are varied. Before 1975, average holding period was higher than four years each and every year. From 1980 onward, the average fell below three years and remained there. In 2005, for the first time, the average holding period was less than one year. At the end of 2010, it had fallen to under three months. The Internet has made trading easier than ever before, explaining a part of the trend since 2000; but the trend predates the Internet, so a broader trend has been underway. It might be related to the timing of major market primary trends. For example, after the 1929 crash, the average holding period rose until 1945, after which the decline began.

Key Point
A long-term trend in the market is for stock holding periods to decline over time. Most recently, the average has fallen below one year for the first time.

Whatever the cause, the value investing philosophy of buy and hold has lost popularity in recent years and activities like day trading have become increasingly popular. This trend might provide clues to what is going to happen in the future. Investors and traders both play a role in influencing long-term price trends of individual stocks and of the entire market; but no one can say with certainty which group will prevail in future years.

Day traders, like long-term investors, understand the adage that *the trend is your friend*. The timeframe, however, is quite different. Buy-and-hold proponents may criticize the extremely short-term mindset of the day trader by expanding the adage to *the trend is your friend—until the end*. In other words, an accumulation of small, rapid profits can be wiped out in one ill-timed move.

SWING TRADING

Day trading and intra-day trading focus intentionally on very short entry-to-exit timeframes. Traders use charts of very small time spans, and may take profits within a matter of moments. In comparison, swing trading uses many of the same short-term trend and reversal signals, but involves a holding period of at least three days, and in most applications, not more than five days.

Swing traders rely on specific *set-up signals* for both entry and exit. Because swing traders are playing the swing of price, the current trend's exit set-up may also serve as the next swing's entry set-up.

There are four important price patterns for swing trading. These are:

1. *Three or more short-term trending days.* A *trend* is a very specific manner under the rules of swing trading. An *uptrend* is a series of consecutive sessions characterized by each session showing a higher high price than the previous session, and also showing a higher low price. These higher highs and higher lows must occur at least over three sessions.

    For example, a three-day series consists of high–low prices of $24–22, $27–23, and $28–25. This is an uptrend because over the three sessions, both the high and low levels increased.

    A *downtrend* is recognized as a series of three or more consecutive sessions characterized by lower highs and lower lows.

    For example, a three-day series consists of high–low prices of $24–22, $23–20, and $21–19. This is a downtrend because over the three sessions, both the high and low levels decreased.

2. An *NRD.* The *narrow range day (NRD)* is one with a trading range with opening and closing prices close to one another. The NRD may be relative to preceding sessions; but the closer the opening and closing prices, the stronger the indication is that a reversal is coming. It indicates that at the end of the trend, the current price is close to agreement between buyers and sellers, or that the trending action has been exhausted.

3. *Exceptionally high volume.* When a *volume spike* occurs, it also signals high chances for a price reversal. The spike occurs for a good reason and may signal that the direction of the existing trend has come to an end, with the other side (buyers versus sellers, or sellers versus buyers) about to take control.

4. *A change in price direction, ending the trend.* When a *reversal day* appears, it clearly ends the trend as defined by swing traders. So a series of upward-moving days concludes with a downward-moving day, or vice versa. This, especially when combined with other reversal signals, is a sign of a broader reversal.

set-up signals

Patterns or changes in price or volume that tell day traders and swing traders when likely trend reversals are about to take place.

uptrend

In swing trading, a series of consecutive sessions with higher high prices and higher low prices in each session, compared to the previous session.

downtrend

In swing trading, a series of consecutive sessions with lower high prices and lower low prices in each session, compared to the previous session.

narrow-range day (NRD)

A trading session in which opening and closing prices are very close or identical, indicating exhausting of the trend and a likely reversal about to occur.

When two or more of these signals occur together, they confirm one another and provide the strongest possible indication that the price is likely to stop moving in the established direction and will probably turn and move in the opposite direction.

> **Key Point**
> As valuable as the reversal signals are that swing traders use, when two or more show up together, the strength of the confirmation is very strong.

The philosophy behind swing trading is based on two observations. First is the basic contrarian strategy. This is the belief that the majority is more often wrong than right. So when prices begin moving upward, a growing number of people buy, with most buyers at the top of the short-term trend. And when prices begin moving downward, a growing number of people sell, with most sellers at the bottom of the short-term trend.

Second is the belief that market decisions are made based on two primary emotions: greed and fear. As prices rise, new buyers come in to get a piece of the action and existing owners of stock do not take profits, because they do not want to miss out on even higher gains. When prices fall, current owners of stock panic and sell, mostly at the bottom of the price swing.

The swing traders acknowledge the strength of greed and fear as motivating forces in the market, but they resist acting in response. They make decisions rationally and without emotion. When greed drives prices up, swing traders look for the signs that the trend is slowing or coming to an end. When that happens, they sell long positions or open short positions. When prices are falling, swing traders wait for signals that the trend is bottoming out. At that point, they buy to close any short positions, or open long positions.

This swing is normally going to last between three and five sessions. Swing traders want to move in and out of positions that quickly, because part of the strategy recognizes that the short-term emotional reaction is always exaggerated; but it also corrects at the end of that three- to five-day period. In fact, it is the emotional reaction and overreaction that creates the short-term swing.

EXIT AND ENTRY SIGNALS

The dilemma most traders are aware of is *when* to enter a position. But there is more. After you enter, you also need to know when and why to exit the position. Both of these decisions can be based on gut reaction (greed and fear dominating), or on a logical assessment of the price for the stock and recognition of the nonemotional reasons for moving.

Just as investors need to set goals for exiting positions based on profit targets or loss bail-out points, traders also need to know when to sell. When you are operating based on one of the several theories of trading, you really are not aware of risk. That awareness only takes hold once real money is placed into a trade. This is why setting very clear entry and exit rules for yourself is essential to trading success.

volume spike

A single trading session with higher-than-average volume, signaling the possibility of a coming reversal of price movement.

Key Point
Even if you understand the steps and techniques of trading, you do not truly appreciate risk until you have actual money committed to a position.

One of the confusing patterns you see time and again is a *congestion* pattern in price. This occurs after a trend has ended and before another trend begins. Congestion can last two or three sessions or for an entire month or more. Prices move sideways without making any clear moves in either direction. Another name for this could be *confusion* because neither buyers nor sellers are in control, and no one can decide which way prices are going to move next.

reversal day

The end of a trend; a session that moves in the direction opposite the established direction, signaling a high possibility of a reversal in the price direction.

congestion

A price pattern of sideways movement within a narrow trading range, with neither buyers nor sellers in control.

During periods of congestion, patterns are going to emerge, giving you a clue about trends about to emerge. It often occurs that traders wait out the congestion hoping to spot a strong trend; but by the time the trend is apparent, the opportunity has been lost. This is a dangerous point in the trend. Some movement away from congestion could end up as a failed signal. The danger of making decisions to either enter or exit positions during periods of congestion is in the difficulty of reading when the period is really ending. The solution is to seek out strong signals of a trend, and to not make a move without equally strong confirmation.

It is better to lose an opportunity because of the dangers in trying to read the congestion pattern than to make a decision and end up losing on the trade. If you consider the patterns taking place right before congestion, the confusion makes sense. It is likely to follow a period of very strong trending price action, even including strong or consecutive price gaps and then exhaustion. At this point, when momentum has been used up, neither buyers nor sellers are able to create movement. This is when failed signals may develop. It isn't so much that the signal is deceptive, but that it lacks the strength to continue in the direction indicated.

Key Point

In periods of congestion, the uncertainty confuses the decision-making process even with signals; you are better off missing an opportunity than risking a loss in these conditions.

Confirmation may come in the form of two or more reversal or entry signals (initiation of a trend of three or more days, an NRD, or a volume spike). Remember, when two or more of these show up together, it is an exceptionally strong indication that prices are about to begin trending. However, today charts are available to everyone with a computer and knowledge about technical analysis is more widespread than ever. This does not necessarily mean that indicators are interpreted accurately; in fact, with the widespread access there is a tendency to oversimplify the meaning of indicators. Trading is not a formula that works every time; you cannot see a signal and act on it with certainty. Rather, the accurate interpretation of technical indicators should improve the frequency of being right, improving your averages rather than creating surefire systems for profitability.

Exit profits can be summarized as percentage gain/loss or dollar amounts. These should be realistic and moderate and, most important, once you set your exit standards, you have to follow your own rules. Otherwise, the exercise contains no value.

Traders make some recurring errors that can be avoided as long as you know about them. These are:

- Trying to make profits on a trade adequate to make up for a loss previously experienced (this increases your risk exposure and usually will not work out profitably).
- Converting small losses into large losses.
- Dwelling on a loss or poorly timed trade rather than learning from it and moving on.
- Setting unrealistic goals, notably excessively high profits, which ensures you will rarely meet those goals.

Key Point
Traders are at risk of making errors in their approach to trades; the solution is to set clear policies and then follow your own rules.

For entry and exit, note the following signals that provide you with the strongest and best action points:

- In all cases, even a strong indicator should be confirmed. This may be a matter of confirming an NRD with a reversal day or volume spike, or seeing a three-session trend coming out of confirmation, along with an NRD.
- Look for gapping action or, as they say in London's Underground subway system, Mind the Gap. Gaps are very significant because they imply that buyers (upside gaps) or sellers (downside gaps) are making their move. Gaps are especially meaningful when they occur as part of a breakout above resistance or below support. However, before jumping in, look for confirmation of a new trend; the gap may reverse and fill, retreating to the established trading range, making it a failed signal.
- Breakouts that hold and continue to move represent a strong signal, assuming confirmation occurs as well by way of gaps, three or more trending sessions, or other strong indicators.
- You are going to create more profits by getting in at the proper moment, which is right after confirmation but before the crowd acts. If you wait, it will be too late. Traders who lead rather than follow are going to have more profits.
- The traditional technical signs, like tests of resistance or support, head and shoulders, and triangles, are confirming patterns but are not as reliable on their own as the swing trade reversal signs (NRDs, volume spikes, and reversal days after short-term trends).

To accurately decide when to enter or exit, you may select from a number of signals and confirmations. However, the ideal indicator is not always going to show up, so an alternative is to look for a percentage of price movement above or below a previous level and use this as the decision point. You decide to buy if the price movement is downward a specific percentage from the high; you sell if the price movement is upward from the low. This *percentage swing* approach provides you with a framework and discipline that programs your decision point; it is based on the observed tendency for price to go through predictable swings in three to five days.

percentage swing

Price movement of a specified percentage below the high or above the low, used to generate entry or exit decisions as part of a swing trading strategy.

Key Point

Using the percentage swing method gives you clear signals for timing entry and exit; this helps overcome confusion and uncertainty, even in volatile markets.

The desirability of percentage swing is that entry and exit are automatic, assuming you follow the rules you establish within the swing. The percentage that you select depends on your risk tolerance as a trader, and on different degrees of change for entry and for exit. For example, if you are out of a swing trade and you use percentage swing to reenter, you may set the percentage at 5 percent or 10 percent. If too high, you may never reach the point; if too low, you might enter too soon. For exit, you might have a greater sensitivity to loss, meaning a loss percentage might be lower than a gain percentage.

Percentage swing is a good system, at least to generate your attention. However, it works best as a first step in the decision, which should not be made until a confirming signal develops. It is possible that a percentage will occur, but the other signals have not developed or you even see a contradictory signal (in technical indicators, candlestick formations, or other methods you employ). In those situations, use percentage swing as one among many different signal points you employ as part of your timing strategies.

true range

A recalculated trading range including not only a single session, but the range between one session's closing price and the next session's high.

gapping behavior

Differences in price levels between one day's closing price and the next day's opening price, especially when this incidence is repetitive or frequent.

> **Key Point**
> Percentage swing is best used as a generating change, but the movement should be confirmed by other indicators before you act.

In calculating the percentage swing, it is not always necessary to restrict the test to the change within a single trading session. In periods of great volatility between sessions, you may calculate and track a stock's *true range* between the previous day's closing price and the current day's high price. This encompasses a range well beyond a single session's opening and closing, and may provide more significant insights in the price movement and the timing of your entry or exit.

True range analysis may absorb the day-to-day *gapping behavior* that otherwise clouds judgment and makes interpretation difficult. Not all gaps are visible, either, so true range analysis helps to clarify the situation especially when price volatility is high. These day-to-day gaps are not always visible. For example, if yesterday's price opened at $26 and closed at $23, and today's price opened at $20 and closed at $24, there was a three-point gap between the two sessions. However, on a candlestick chart the two sessions overlap, so the gap is not as visible as one in which both sessions move in the same direction.

It also helps to see gaps if you combine daily sessions with higher-volume interim charts. For example, you might see frequent gaps on a one-hour chart that do not show up at all in the full-day chart. This does not mean the day's session is any more volatile than average; it does provide you with insight about trading action during the session rather than the summarized range information for the entire day. In the true range version of a trading range, the high price is either today's high or yesterday's close, and the low is either today's low or yesterday's close. This system applies in looking backward on daily charts, or in performing the same function on one-hour or even more frequent charts during the day.

Key Point

Gapping behavior may be invisible, not only between sessions but even within a single session; combining daily charts with higher-frequency charts like one-hour or 20-minute charts helps spot volatility within the session.

Regardless of the duration of your sessions, it is important to understand that gapping behavior affects the conclusions you draw. For example, in a percentage swing, do you use today's opening price as your point of comparison? Or do you use yesterday's closing price? If these have gapped overnight, the analysis could be rendered inaccurate if you limit it to the current session only.

The real key to ensuring your analysis of price movement is accurate interpretation of charts. The next chapter explores charting and the many tools you can find in single-session or multiple-session trends.

TO BE CONTINUED...

11 CHARTING TOOLS & INTERPRETATION

Traders rely on charts. They study and analyze charts not only to spot price trends, but also to decide when to enter or exit a position. This is the key to trading. It is not enough to identify a stock that you like, or that you believe is going to move in the direction you desire. You also need to determine precisely when to enter a position and when to exit.

This is no small matter. It takes considerable study and analysis to develop a sense of the many timing signals that you need and will use to improve the timing of trades. These set-up signals can include a short-term trend as it begins or ends, volume levels, traditional technical signs like gaps and breakouts from the established trading range, and specific price patterns you find on charts.

Key Point
Entry and exit timing signals are numerous and not always easy to spot. It requires experience and practice to fine-tune the skill traders rely upon to time their trading decisions.

candlesticks

Chart entries based on rectangular boxes that show at a glance the opening and closing price, trading range, and direction of price movement for a trading session.

Japanese candlesticks

Alternative name for candlesticks and for the charts on which they are used.

Technical indicators are keys to improving your chart-based analysis. The premise of this range of tools rests with the trading range and well-defined levels of support and resistance. More specifically, conclusions are reached by how price acts and tests these trading range borders. The technical indicators based on the theory of trading range patterns are collectively called *Western technical indicators* and are based on interpretations traditionally performed through the development of charts over a period of days, weeks, and months. They focus on price and volume changes and developing levels of momentum. This chapter is focused specifically on various kinds of charts that you will use to study price patterns and improve your timing.

Before the widespread use of the Internet and easy access to free and instantaneous online charting, traders had to build their own charts by plotting prices each day and hoping to identify opportunities to enter positions or changing trends to generate well-timed exits. By today's standards, these old-style methods are quite primitive. Today, traders are more likely to use *Eastern technical indicators*. This is a method of analysis and timing based on the study of *candlestick* charting.

This chapter explains various types of charts and then focuses on how candlesticks, also called *Japanese candlesticks*, are used effectively not only to improve what charts reveal, but provide patterns in single sessions, double sessions, and triple sessions that reveal likely price direction about to occur.

TRADITIONAL TYPES OF CHARTS

Candlestick charts would be very difficult to use if you had to construct them by hand for a long series of trading sessions. The Internet has changed all of that, making charts of all kinds easy to tailor and instantly available.

Key Point

The Internet has made trading fast, efficient, and easy. However, this means that the potential for losses is equally fast, efficient, and easy. The Internet does not ensure profits; it exposes you to greater potential *and* to greater danger.

Before the modern era, traders relied on services to provide charts to them or they had to build them by hand. The most basic kind of chart is the *line chart*, which is simply a line tracking a stock's value over time. The value used is usually the day's ending price.

A typical line chart is shown in Figure 11.1. This is a chart for three months for Home Depot (HD).

This chart provides you with a very simple summary of the sequence of closing prices on each session. As a broad overview of Home Depot's price history, this is useful; but it does not provide any useful intelligence about the trend within the price, or of what is likely to happen next. For this you need to be able to analyze each day's opening and closing price as well as the complete trading range (the range usually includes some movement above and below the opening and closing levels).

line chart

A simplified chart for tracking a stock's price, consisting of a single line connected between days, and normally reflecting the stock's closing price for each session.

Key Point

The value of charted information is important because you need to see not only the current price, but how that has changed from session to session and within each session.

HD (Home Depot, Inc.) NYSE
30-Dec-2011   Open 42.15 High 42.32 Low 42.01 Last 42.04 Volume 4.8M Chg +0.03 (+0.07%) ▲
© StockCharts.com
— HD (Daily) 42.04   42.04

Figure 11.1 Home Depot (HD), Line Chart
Source: Stockcharts.com.

OHLC chart

A stock chart showing each session's trading range by way of a vertical stick, as well as opening and closing price noted by small horizontal sticks.

The same history of Home Depot, but in OHLC format, is shown in Figure 11.2. Although the history is identical, the detail is much greater on the OHLC than on the relatively simple line chart. The vertical stick on each session represents the full trading range for the day. The small horizontal protrusion on the left is the opening price, and the one on the right is the closing price. The distance in between these two is the breadth of the day, or the distance between opening and closing.

When the closing price is higher than the opening price, the session moved upward; when lower, the session moved downward. The nice feature of the *OHLC chart* is that it is very simple but provides all of the information that you need. The main disadvantage is that spotting trends or significant patterns is quite difficult.

Key Point

The OHLC chart is an efficient but rudimentary way to pick up all of a session's important information, but it is not visually easy to track price or to spot short-term trends.

Both line chart and OHLC provide some level of information, but today the most popular chart is the candlestick chart. This provides all that you need, at a glance, to identify not only the trading range but also the direction of price movement for each session and within a multisession trend.

Figure 11.2 Home Depot (HD), OHLC Chart

Source: Stockcharts.com.

CANDLESTICK CHARTS: THE BASICS

The candlestick conveys a great amount of information in a relatively simple shape: a triangle with a "wick" above, below, or on both ends. The same Home Depot chart in candlestick form is shown in Figure 11.3.

The features of the candlestick include the *real body*, which is the rectangle. If it is white or clear, the session moved upward; if it is black, the session moved downward. The advantage to this feature should be obvious; you can immediately spot trends over a series of sessions when the color of the real body is the same during the period.

The sticks above or below the real body represent the full trading range of the day. The upper and lower horizontal lines of the triangle represent the opening and closing prices; the body itself is the distance between opening and closing. The sticks above and below the real body are the complete trading range for the day. These are called the *shadows* and are also called *tails* when exceptionally long, or *wicks*. The tail form of a shadow often has extra significance because it represents a failed attempt to move price farther than the opening/closing range.

real body

The middle rectangle of a candlestick, showing whether the session moved upward (white) or downward (black), and making it possible to spot trends immediately.

Figure 11.3 Home Depot (HD), Candlestick Chart

Source: Stockcharts.com.

The shadows are given additional names that tell you whether price moved above or below the real body. The *upper shadow* represents price action that was bullish, or an attempt to move prices higher even though the day's prices closed below that level. The *lower shadow* is the range of prices below the real body, or an attempt to move prices lower that failed, and with prices returning to the real body before the end of the session.

The complete candlestick shows you not only direction for the sessions, but for a range of sessions. The different segments of the candlestick are shown in Figure 11.4.

Referring back to the Home Depot candlestick chart in Figure 11.3, how much can you discover from this chart? This period began with a nice uptrend including some gapping patterns. It ended with a middle period of sideways movement, or congestion, in which neither buyers nor sellers had control. This lasted nearly a full month, from the middle of March until the middle of April. The uptrend then resumed.

shadows

The portion of a candlestick above or below the real body, representing the extent of trading range beyond opening and closing prices.

tails

Alternative name for a candlestick's shadows, especially when longer than average.

wicks

Alternative name for a candlestick's shadows.

Figure 11.4 Candlestick Segments

Key Point

A comparison between the same data on an OHLC chart and a candlestick chart demonstrates the vast difference and shows that candlesticks are easier to use and interpret.

Notice the fourth day of the uptrend. It was accompanied by very high volume, confirming the resumption of a bullish trend. Another very clear signal occurred at the very top of the uptrend. The narrow range day (NRD) at the very top is given the name *doji* in candlestick analysis. The word *doji* means "mistake" and it is easy to spot. The distance between opening and closing prices is very small or those levels are identical. So instead of a rectangle, a doji session is a horizontal line.

In the case of Home Depot (Figure 11.3), the doji at the very top of the uptrend was a clear reversal signal. Note the upper shadow, which was an attempt to move price further upward. Its failure signals a loss of momentum and a high likelihood of a reversal and price decline.

While there are dozens of candlestick formations that provide excellent insight into price movement, momentum, continuation, and reversal, following are some of the major ones worth paying attention to. These recur often at key points in a price trend and may signal reversal and to confirm what other indicators also reveal.

Key Point

There are so many specific candlestick formations that they are rich analytical tools; at the same time it takes practice and study to master the range of indicators in the form of candlestick sessions.

The first group worth analyzing is the single-stick candle. This is a candlestick of a single day that holds special meaning and also provides valuable insight about the current trend. Single-stick formations include the following:

upper shadow

The vertical portion of a candlestick extending above the real body and representing a failed attempt during the session to move the price higher.

lower shadow

The vertical portion of a candlestick extending below the real body and representing a failed attempt during the session to move the price lower.

doji

A candlestick with little or no distance between opening and closing, so that a horizontal line is found instead of a rectangle.

Long candles. A *long candle* is any candlestick, white or black, with an exceptionally wide breadth between opening and closing price. A long white candle appearing at or near the bottom of a downtrend is a strong reversal signal; it shows that buyers controlled price action throughout the day. A long black candle showing up at the top of an uptrend has the same meaning, a likely reversal and start of a downtrend.

The long candle may also appear in the middle of a trend. If the color of the candle is consistent with the trend direction (white in uptrends or black in downtrends), it may serve as a *continuation day* or indicator.

A variation of the long candle is the *marubozu.* In Japanese, this word means "little hair." It is called this because it is a long candle with one of three features: It either has no shadows, or only an upper shadow, or only a lower shadow.

The marubozu with neither shadow is the strongest sign of a bullish trend (white marubozu) or a bearish trend (black marubozu).

The long candlestick types are summarized in Figure 11.5.

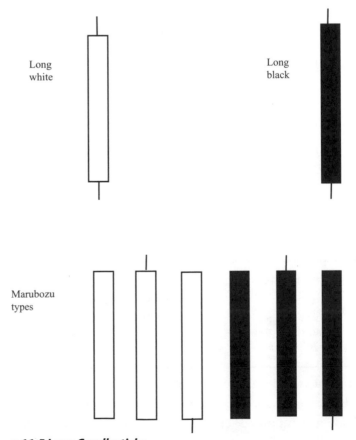

Figure 11.5 Long Candlesticks

Short candles. On the opposite side of the scale of single-day candles is the short candle. The extreme version of this is the previously mentioned doji, which comes in several varieties. Every doji consists of a horizontal line instead of a rectangular real body; the opening and closing price for the session is identical or extremely close together. A *dragonfly doji* has a lower shadow, so it forms a capital letter T. The extent of the lower shadow determines the strength; the lower the shadow, the stronger. If a dragonfly doji shows up at the bottom of the trend, it is extremely bullish because the attempted move downward failed.

The opposite of the dragonfly is the *gravestone doji*, which has only an upper shadow and looks like a capital T turned upside down. When this appears at the top of an uptrend, it is a very strong reversal indicator.

The short candlestick types are summarized in Figure 11.6.

Dragonfly doji

Gravestone doji

Figure 11.6 Short Candlesticks

Trend-based candles. Some single-stick candles have a meaning that relies on the current market conditions. These are bullish, bearish, and sideways. So a specific candlestick might appear but its interpretation relies on these conditions.

Key Point
A general observation about candlesticks: Exceptionally long and exceptionally short real bodies are probably the most significant signals you are going to see.

The first among these is the *long-legged doji*, which has exceptionally long upper *and* lower shadows. The horizontal real body appears closer to the middle of the overall formation.

A long-legged doji showing up at the top of an uptrend signals possible reversal and is bearish; when it shows up at the bottom of a downtrend, it is bullish and may signal a coming uptrend. However, the long-legged doji (like any pattern) may also fail and in hindsight could be a misleading indicator. This is why all patterns in candlestick analysis need to be confirmed before entry or exit decisions are finalized.

Key Point

Some candlestick sessions, like the long-legged doji, may be either bullish or bearish depending on where they show up.

Another candle that depends on where it shows up is the *spinning top*. This is a candle with a small real body of either color, and long upper and lower shadows. It is similar to the long-legged doji, and like the doji, the spinning top's real body should appear about halfway through the formation.

A spinning top is a buy signal when it shows up at the bottom of a downtrend, or a sell signal at the top of an uptrend. Reversal works in both conditions and the important feature is placement along with shape; the color of the real body is incidental.

Key Point

A spinning top candlestick, like the long-legged doji, may be bullish or bearish. It depends on where it appears.

A final single-stick development that appears a lot is the *hammer* or *hanging man*. These both consist of a small real body (color does not matter) and a long lower shadow with no upper shadow. When this shows up at the bottom of a downtrend, it is a bullish reversal signal and is called a hammer. If it shows up at the top of an uptrend, it is a bearish reversal and is called a hanging man.

The trend-based candlestick types are summarized in Figure 11.7.

Two-stick patterns. Another group of candlesticks worth noting involves two consecutive sessions. The *engulfing pattern* consists of a set-up day that has a smaller rectangle on both sides, with the second day's real body extending beyond. The second day's high is higher, and its low is lower than the day preceding. The bullish version consists of a black set-up session and a white second session; the bearish version is the opposite, with a white set-up and black second session.

Another two-stick pattern is called a *harami*. In Japanese, this word means "pregnant." This is the opposite of the engulfing pattern and consists of a set-up day that has a higher high and a higher low than the second day. A bullish version has a black set-up and a white second day; and a bearish version has a white set-up day and a black second day.

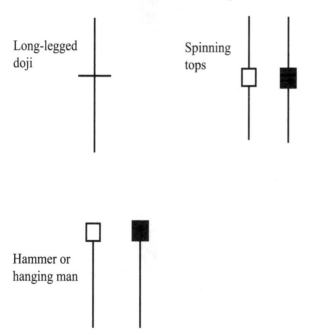

Figure 11.7 Trend-Based Candlesticks

Dozens of additional two-stick patterns also can be used for reversal signals, confirmation, and continuation indicators. The preceding are only the most prominent and widely used among them.

Key Point
There are dozens of two-stick candlestick indicators. Some are more subtle than others; they provide excellent forms of initial indicators or confirmation signals.

The two-stick candlestick types are summarized in Figure 11.8.

Three-stick patterns. The most complex but also the strongest of candle-stick indicators are made up of three consecutive sessions. There are dozens of these and, like the single- and double-stick patterns, the following are only the most easily found and most common of the three-stick patterns.

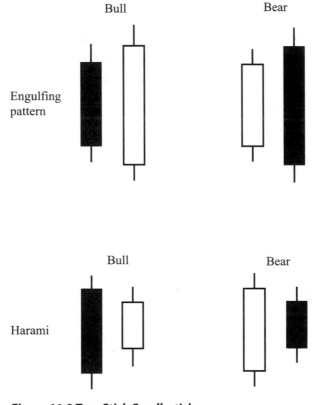

Figure 11.8 Two-Stick Candlesticks

First is the *three white soldiers*, which involves three days with all white candles that each move higher. To qualify, the closing price of each session has to be higher than the previous, *and* the opening price (the bottom of the real body) also has to be higher than the previous day's opening price.

Key Point
Three-stick indicators are the strongest of all. Because there are three consecutive sessions in each pattern, they serve as a mini-trend of their own.

The opposite of the bullish three white soldiers is the bearish *three black crows* pattern. This is a series of black candles. Each day's opening price is lower than the previous day's open, and each closing is lower than the previous day's close.

Another interesting three-day pattern is the *squeeze alert*. A bullish version looks like the three black crows with an important difference. All three sessions are black, but each day's range is lower on both sides. Each reports a lower high and a higher low. The bearish squeeze alert is the opposite and it is similar to the three white soldiers. However, each session's high is lower than the previous; and each session's low is higher than the previous.

The three-stick candlestick types are summarized in Figure 11.9.

Many additional candlesticks are found in the study of charts, and work well to confirm indicated reversal and continuation patterns. The preceding is only an introductory look at candlesticks. The range of possible signals is vast, with more than 100 potential different signals consisting of single sticks or two-day or three-day formations.

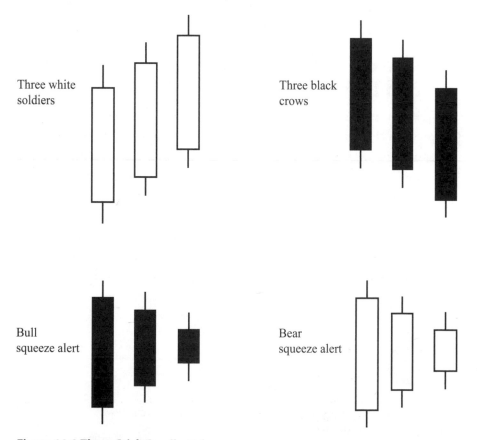

Three white soldiers

Three black crows

Bull squeeze alert

Bear squeeze alert

Figure 11.9 Three-Stick Candlesticks

COMBINING CANDLESTICKS WITH WESTERN TECHNICAL ANALYSIS

The concept of confirmation has been introduced and explained in previous chapters. However, it is more than the verification of what appears to be taking place by seeing the same thing through a second indicator. Confirmation, especially for the timing of entry and exit, involves much more.

Candlesticks—including one-, two-, and three-session patterns—are reliable initial indicators for change in price patterns, especially reversal. So, for example, a day trader or swing trader can use candlesticks to improve timing. Relying on reversal days, NRDs, and volume spikes can be effective as a timing management tool, but when these are combined with candlestick analysis, the technique is far more powerful.

Key Point
Candlesticks are not stand-alone indicators, but part of a wider system of confirmation between candlesticks and other technical methods.

In that sense, confirmation does include two or more independent indicators pointing in the same direction; but it also is made more effective by being put into action as a cross-disciplinary tool. So candlesticks, which are Eastern, are effectively employed with the traditional Western signals that chartists and day or swing traders rely upon. This can work in either direction. An initial indicator may be Eastern or Western and then be confirmed by the other side.

This makes candlestick charting very effective as part of a broader timing strategy. In addition to verification by way of two or more signals, the independent sources and theories of how those signals develop strengthen the confirmation.

The key to Western technical theories is the basic support and resistance that define the current trading range, and the way that price patterns approach these borders, break through them, continue or retreat, and create or lose momentum. The next chapter summarizes the essential tools of technical analysis; remember, however, that these are going to be most effective when used along with candlestick chart patterns as forms of confirmation.

201

TO BE CONTINUED...

12 ESSENTIAL TECHNICAL INDICATORS

The topic of technical analysis has filled many books that still only scratched the surface. This chapter is by no means an exhaustive explanation of the entire realm of technical analysis; however, it does provide a summary of the most important concepts and indicators that technical analysts rely upon to analyze price movement.

The difference between fundamental and technical analysis is a good starting point for understanding how it all works. Both disciplines are most effective when used together because each side approaches analysis from a different perspective. The collective insights you gain by combining the fundamental and the technical are more useful than either analytical school of thought can provide alone.

Key Point
Fundamental and technical analyses begin from different starting points, making them most valuable when used together.

Technical analysis relies on the study of price patterns and trends of stocks. Fundamental analysis relies on the study of historical financial results and capitalization of companies. Both are intended to help select companies and their stocks, even though they come to the question with vastly different assumptions. Because fundamental science is historical and focused on the company, it is the favored technique for investors. This contrasts with traders, who focus on timing of entry and exit in positions in the short term, with little focus on long-term investment value or comparative quality of the company itself.

Examples

A Question of Preferences: One investor relies on long-term historical trends like revenues and earnings, debt ratio, and dividend yield. These basic fundamental indicators are very popular. A second investor prefers watching price patterns and seeking price and momentum signals foreshadowing changes in direction. This is a technical approach. A third investor combines both disciplines and watches both fundamental and technical indicators to judge price value as well as financial strength.

It is not only possible, but wise, for an individual to devote a share of the overall portfolio to each side. Thus, you build a long-term portfolio of stocks based on the principles of value investing, and you also use a portion of capital for short-term trading based on current market conditions and the rise and fall of prices. In order to accomplish this two-part strategic method, you need to understand the basics of both sides. Following are the highlights of basic technical analysis every trader needs to master.

SUPPORT AND RESISTANCE: THE TRADING RANGE AS A DEFINING ATTRIBUTE OF PRICE

Most traders have heard about support and resistance; but few truly understand how significant it is and how it serves as the basis for virtually every technical indicator.

When you go through a list of technical signs and signals, you discover that most of them are given importance based on how they interact with support and resistance. These defining borders of the trading range provide a sense of order and predictability to analysis. When price levels remain within the trading range, it leads to a specific conclusion; when price breaks out above resistance or below support, it leads to a completely different conclusion.

Key Point
Practically all technical indicators are based on a comparison between price action and support and resistance.

A price breakout may retreat to the previously established trading range. If that occurs, it is likely to take place fairly quickly after the breakout. If price continues to move above or below the previous range, it probably means a new trading range is being set.

When price moves out of the current trading range, how do you decide where the new borders should be set? For some traders, the violation of a trading range leads to a period of chaos and uncertainty. Until a new, clearly defined border is set, they cannot rely on price trends. However, an interesting phenomenon occurs in some instances, in which the previous level of resistance becomes the new level of support, or the previous support becomes the new resistance.

This *range flip* can be used to set a new test for subsequent price movement. If the newly observed resistance or support is later violated in a price reversal, it means the new level of trading will not hold. If the new level is tested but prices remain within its border, it means the newly set range is permanent.

For example, the chart for Boeing (BA) in Figure 12.1 demonstrates how this flip takes place and how it appears.

range flip

The observed change after a price breakout, in which previous resistance becomes new support in an uptrend, or in which previous support becomes new resistance in a downtrend.

In this example, prices moved above the resistance level and remained there. The previous resistance became new support and although the price level remained close to that line, it did not break through. In some cases of breakout, price will quickly return back to previous levels. The fact that the new support level held indicates strength in the new trading range.

Key Point

The tendency for support and resistance to flip after a successful price breakout is an important clue for traders; this helps add confidence in new trading levels, or to test whether the breakout is going to succeed or fail.

Figure 12.1 Range Flip, Resistance to Support
Source: Stockcharts.com.

Another example is found in the three-month chart of the same period for SPDR Gold Trust (GLD), as shown in Figure 12.2. This is an example of previous support flipping over to new resistance.

GLD's support level held up for over two months before prices fell below. The gap marked the breakout but at this point, traders could not know whether the breakout would hold. They had to rely on the newly set resistance level, which was slightly lower than prior support. The price trend did appear toward the end of the chart to be strongly bearish. Although the price tested the $160 level briefly in January, prices retreated and remained below that level as of mid-month.

The established trading levels define *volatility*, another name for market risk. The wider the trading range breadth, the greater the volatility; and the more often a breakout occurs (even if prices eventually retreat), the less certainty a trader can have in the price trend. This is especially true if the price history includes many gaps. The bigger the gaps, the more volatile the price and the less predictable the future.

The trading borders are so crucial to most types of technical analysis because price levels take on meaning when these borders are tested. When you review any form of price pattern, you have to be aware of how it interacts with support or resistance, and what it means when price either breaks through or fails to break through. A failed breakout is most often interpreted as the last thing to occur before prices begin a strong move in the opposite direction. In other words, if sellers try to move price down and fail, it is likely that buyers are going to gain momentum and successfully move price higher, and vice versa. This interaction between sellers and buyers is constant and unending, and every trend eventually loses momentum and turns.

These trading range borders also can be defined as the locations where supply and demand are tested and determined, at least within the moment. No current trading range, no matter how firmly held, is going to be permanent. Stock prices are dynamic and will eventually move away from the trading range, either up or down. From the supply and demand side, the forces affecting prices as well as the trading range borders are clearly defined.

Figure 12.2 Range Flip, Support to Resistance
Source: Stockcharts.com.

Key Point
A rule of opposite movement applies consistently to trading patterns. After a failure to break through one side, prices invariably move in the opposite direction.

When more traders want to buy, prices are driven up due to more demand than supply; when more sellers want to sell, prices are driven down due to more supply than demand. This oversimplifies the process in a sense, because many influences affect prices beyond the simple forces of supply and demand. These forces include momentary perceptions of value, opinions about a company, earnings reports versus analysts' estimates, mergers and acquisitions, rumors, lawsuits, product recalls or new product announcements, changes in management, and any other important change or belief about a coming change within a company.

Support is the bottom of the trading range. But more specifically, it is the price level where further decline is unlikely, where buyers consider the price attractive and also where sellers are willing to make trades. Below that level, demand becomes too strong for prices to continue downward because buyers perceive the support level as a good price and anything below that would be a bargain. Demand offsets and even surpasses supply at the support level, which prevents further price decline.

If prices do fall below support, it means that sellers have prevailed. Selling expectations are lower and buyers are not interested, perhaps due to weaker than expected earnings, the perception that the stock is priced too high, or a cyclical negative opinion about the industry that comes from economic change. However, support levels rarely go into a freefall except in a market panic. At some point, the price is going to become cheap enough that buyers will once again want to buy shares. That point sets a new level of support.

Because prices may trade briefly below the established support price, traders acknowledge a *support zone* in place of a specific price. This is done because prices may dip below support temporarily. On a candlestick chart, you often see a closing price at or above support, but with the session's trading below that level. This *testing of the waters* below support may come from an attempted bearish breakout, or simply as a momentary trading glitch that does not last.

Resistance is the opposite of support, or the top of the current trading range. It is the price at which prices are not likely to rise any farther because buyers lack the momentum; put another way, sellers consider the resistance price to be acceptable, but anything above that price would be an inflated value. And so resistance holds for the moment as an agreed-upon price. Buyers are not willing to pay more per share than the resistance price.

Putting this in supply and demand terms, as price levels rise to resistance, sellers are more likely to sell and take profits, and buyers are less likely to buy because the price is relatively high.

A breakout above resistance may be permanent, in which case a new trading range will be set. Prices will not rise indefinitely; at some point, momentum slows down and a new resistance level is established. A breakout may also fail to hold, and prices will retreat to the established trading range. In those instances where prices are especially volatile at or near resistance, traders may set a *resistance zone* instead of a specific price. This is a small price range where resistance holds, but trading may move above the price briefly.

support zone

A range of prices representing support, used in place of a single price.

resistance zone

A range of prices representing resistance, used in place of a single price.

Key Point

To best understand how the trading borders define price movement, they have to be interpreted in terms of how buyers and sellers view specific price levels.

The nature and volatility of trading within the trading range often defines the strength or weakness of the current resistance and support levels. The trading that takes place within the defined range is called the *channel*. This price movement may remain in a small range or bounce off of both resistance and support while remaining within the borders.

When the channels continue in a sideways pattern for an extended period of time, it indicates that the forces of supply and demand (between buyers and sellers) are evenly matched.

channel

Trading within the bounds of resistance and support, which does not break through on either side.

The trading range can be firmly set with fixed price levels, and with trading taking place within that range; or it may be dynamic. In a dynamic trading range, the channel moves either upward or downward and both resistance and support rise or fall. However, the breadth remains approximately the same. So the range is defined by its breadth rather than by a fixed price at the top or at the bottom.

An example of a sideways-moving channel was seen in the three-month chart for Altria (MO) shown in Figure 12.3.

The channel ends with prices breaking to the upside, appearing to set a new trading range by the conclusion of the charted period. In fact, prices did remain between $28 and $30 through the middle of January. In some sideways channels, price levels will break strongly to the upside or downside; in this instance, the upward move in price was tentative and not especially strong. This could be seen as a signal of low momentum, meaning the uptrend might not be destined to last for long.

Key Point

The trading range is not always fixed in terms of fixed prices; it can also be represented by a trend upward or downward, but with approximately the same fixed breadth.

The channel may also trend upward, as in the case of Exxon Mobil (XOM), shown in Figure 12.4. In this chart, the breadth is quite narrow, only three points from bottom to top, but the trend is clearly upward for one full month. The price rose 12 points in this month without any change in the breadth.

In a downward-trending channel, the same observation can be made. In the case of AT&T (T), which is shown in Figure 12.5, a downward channel moved quickly but the breadth remained at under one point.

Channels allow you to observe the strict and often narrow breadth of the trading range even in periods when prices are trending. These examples prove that it is possible to witness a strong uptrend or downtrend while continuing to observe the limitations of a dynamic trading range.

Figure 12.3 Channels, Sideways Movement
Source: Stockcharts.com.

Figure 12.4 Channels, Upward Movement
Source: Stockcharts.com.

Figure 12.5 Channels, Downward Movement

Source: Stockcharts.com.

POPULAR PRICE PATTERNS AND THEIR MEANINGS

The trading range of a stock provides order and the basis for testing potential later price movement. Following are some of the most popular and useful technical patterns and trends used by traders.

The *head and shoulders* is a very well-known and often-observed pattern. It contains three price spikes. The first and third (shoulders) are lower than the middle (head), and the head is a test of an upward movement. However, because all three spikes retreat, the price is expected to then trend lower. So the three-part test of upward movement fails.

Key Point

The head-and-shoulders pattern is a reliable one because it involves a three-part failed test of resistance. This is most likely to lead to a decline after the pattern develops.

For example, the chart for JPMorgan Chase (JPM) in Figure 12.6 shows a head and shoulders pattern that tests the resistance at about $34.50, with the head moving above that level and then immediately retreating. This is followed by a strong price decline. Toward the end of the chart, price levels recover to the previously established resistance level seen before the head and shoulders occurred.

A head and shoulders is usually going to test resistance without breaking through. In this case, the assumed resistance was broken very briefly, and that failed breakout added to the downward momentum in the reaction trend that followed.

An opposite pattern is the *reverse head and shoulders*, which is identical except that the spikes approach or pass support in an attempt to drive prices downward, and the reaction is for prices to trend upward.

An example of the reverse head and shoulders occurred in the three-month chart of Apple (AAPL) shown in Figure 12.7. In this case, the pattern developed after a downtrend ending with a short breakout below support. The reverse head and shoulders acted just as expected, with prices then breaking into an uptrend that moved strongly for a month.

These patterns do not have to be perfect or even especially strong for their meaning to provide good signals. With all indicators, the stronger the pattern, the better the information it provides. However, in these examples of the head-and-shoulders pattern—which involves three separate price spikes—even a relatively weak pattern is worth observing, especially if it is also confirmed by other indicators.

Figure 12.6 Head and Shoulders
Source: Stockcharts.com.

Figure 12.7 Reverse Head and Shoulders

Source: Stockcharts.com.

Key Point

Any technical pattern may vary in its strength or weakness. It is a mistake to wait for a perfect or classic example, when a relatively weak pattern has the same significance in predicting price developments.

The whole pattern of short-term trends and confirmed reversals involves constant testing of resistance and support. Review charts over several months to spot how these borders hold their importance even long after interim trends have developed and ended.

Beyond the head-and-shoulders pattern are additional patterns that test resistance and support. A variation of testing resistance is the *double top*. In this formation, prices test resistance twice and then retreat in the opposite direction. The double top is an especially strong bearish development because it demonstrates the significance of resistance when it holds; price not only backs away but tends to fall dramatically after the double top.

The double top may occur after an uptrend or at the conclusion of a sideways movement. For example, as shown in Figure 12.8, Intel Corp. (INTC) saw a double top after an uptrend, and in the middle, prices retreated before rising again. However, after the second attempt at further upward movement, prices retreated once again.

The opposite pattern is the *double bottom*, which involves two tests of support followed by a reversal and an uptrend. This occurs either after a downtrend or during a sideways movement when buyers and sellers are struggling for control.

> **Key Point**
> Double tops and bottoms are good ways to spot failed breakout attempts, and to anticipate price movement in the opposite direction.

triangle

A trend involving changes in the breadth of the trading range. As the range narrows during the current trend direction, the likelihood of reversal increases.

The General Mills (GIS) chart showed an example of this, as seen in Figure 12.9. After the double bottom, prices rose but could not be sustained. Price levels finally retreated once again to the level before the double bottom occurred.

Technical analysis is all about patterns, as the head and shoulders and double tops/bottoms reveal. However, it is not only the price level that holds significance to traders, but changes in the breadth of the trading range itself. When the breadth narrows over a series of sessions, it provides a clue of a coming reversal. So the *triangle* is a pattern of declining breadth, and it should not be ignored.

When you see an *ascending triangle*, which occurs during an uptrend, it often means a reversal will occur when the breadth reaches a very narrow point. It consists of flat resistance and rising support.

Bank of America (BAC)'s chart included an example of an ascending triangle lasting about one month, and this is shown in Figure 12.10. This pattern ends with a sizable downside gap and then a strong downtrend. The gap confirmed what the ascending triangle indicated.

Figure 12.8 Double Top

Source: Stockcharts.com.

Figure 12.9   Double Bottom

Source: Stockcharts.com.

Key Point
Confirmation vastly improves a trader's accuracy in predictive analysis. For example, when a triangle occurs along with an engulfing pattern, those are two strong clues that prices are going to reverse.

Figure 12.10   Ascending Triangle

Source: Stockcharts.com.

The opposite pattern, the *descending triangle*, involves a flat support and declining resistance. As the breadth shrinks, the expectation of reversal and uptrend is strong.

An example was seen in the case of General Electric (GE), as shown in Figure 12.11. This gradually declining breadth was typical of a pattern taking place just before reversal and an uptrend.

GE (General Electric Co.) NYSE 30-Dec-2011   **Open** 18.03 **High** 18.08 **Low** 17.88 **Close** 17.91 **Volume** 31.4M **Chg** -0.16 (-0.89%) ▼   © StockCharts.com

Figure 12.11 Descending t Triangle
Source: Stockcharts.com.

TREND LINES FOR SPOTTING REVERSALS

To spot and identify a reversal point, or to confirm that reversal is about to occur, the *trend line* is a very important technical tool. This is a straight line drawn underneath rising support, or above falling resistance. When price turns and interrupts the line, it indicates that a reversal has begun.

Key Point

Trend lines are simple, easy to spot, and provide a clear signal that a trend has ended.

trend line

A straight line drawn beneath a rising support level or above a falling resistance level. Once price levels reverse and interrupt the line, a reversal may be indicated or confirmed.

An example of a trend line occurring during an uptrend was seen in the case of Chevron (CVX), shown in Figure 12.12. Prices continued moving upward strongly for one month. The trend line, drawn beneath the rising support, showed exactly where the uptrend ended and reversed.

The opposite trend line, tracking falling resistance levels in a downtrend, is just as easy to spot and just as strong in locating or confirming a reversal and then a subsequent uptrend. For example, the chart of Microsoft (MSFT) seen in Figure 12.13 tracked a sharp price decline from $27 down to below $24.50 over one week.

Figure 12.12 Trend Line, Uptrend

Source: Stockcharts.com.

Figure 12.13 Trend Line, Downtrend

Source: Stockcharts.com.

The trend line is a strong indicator and it is easy to develop and follow. This makes it one of the best indicators around. The combination of clarity and simplicity is difficult to beat. Trend lines confirm what other indicators also seem to indicate in reversal patterns.

BREAKOUTS AND GAPS

When price levels move above resistance or below support, the change is significant. However, a momentary breakout can also retreat back into the previous trading range, meaning that the breakout fails. When a breakout is accompanied by a gap, the chances of its reversing and filling are quite high. It's all a matter of momentum. If prices move too high too fast, you have to expect a reversal.

Key Point

Both breakouts and gaps can be very meaningful. But when they occur together, smart traders know they have to pay close attention to price movement.

When the breakout moves above resistance, many changes can occur. For example, in Figure 12.14, United Parcel Service (UPS) stock broke through resistance; if you began to analyze the price pattern based on the previously mentioned concept of old resistance becoming new support, that level was tested almost immediately.

Figure 12.14 Breakout Above Resistance

Source: Stockcharts.com.

When breakout occurs below support, the ultimate test is whether or not the breakout will hold. Prices may turn and move back into the previous range. For example, Procter & Gamble (PG) stock went through a downside breakout that lasted slightly longer than one month before prices moved rapidly higher. This is seen in Figure 12.15.

Breakouts are revealing, especially when they occur as part of a gapping action. Several gaps were present on IBM's chart as shown in Figure 12.16.

Figure 12.15 Breakout Below Support

Source: Stockcharts.com.

Key Point

Not all gaps are visible. Detailed analysis reveals that some of the most important gapping patterns involve gaps between up and down days, and these may be shielded because candlestick real bodies overlap.

common gap

A price gap occurring as a part of normal trading activity and without any signal value for changes in the existing trend.

Gaps occur often in most charts. The gap that simply occurs as a matter of normal trading but without any special signal attached is called a *common gap*.

Gaps are important in many different ways. The *breakaway gap* can be subtle and small like the one in the previous chart, or it can be very strong and wide. Its characteristic is that it moves price away from the established trading range.

When a rally takes off strongly, it is also likely to exhaust more quickly. This is not always the case, but on average you may expect to see a quick rally turn suddenly. This is especially true when the trend is accompanied by the *runaway gap* pattern. This is a recurring series of gaps, including consecutive gaps in two or more sessions. This is troubling because of the singular movement without slowing down, and the gapping action may drive price levels much higher or lower than the level justified by actual buyer or seller interest.

Figure 12.16 Gaps

Source: Stockcharts.com.

breakaway gap

A type of gap that moves prices above or below the trading range and either begins a rally or retreats back to the previous level in subsequent sessions.

runaway gap

A pattern of gapping action involving several sessions in close proximity, as part of a trend moving strongly in one direction without offsetting price movement.

Key Point
The runaway gap pattern can be encouraging if prices are going in the direction you want. However, they also mean that the trend is likely to lose momentum quickly and reverse more strongly than trends without these gaps.

Another kind of gap is called the *exhaustion gap*, and this is found at the end of a trend. After a particularly strong trend with a pattern of runaway gaps, exhaustion gaps are more likely than in other trends, and may be seen right as the price direction has turned.

The many types of popular price patterns are useful not so much by themselves but as part of a greater pattern *and* assuming that two or more indicators confirm the apparent significance of current price positions.

Beyond price patterns tracked over a series of sessions, more advanced indicators provide additional confirmation (or contradiction) and provide greater insight. These enable you to anticipate reversals before most traders know they are going to occur.

MOVING AVERAGES, OSCILLATORS, AND VOLUME TESTS

Advanced technical indicators include dozens of tests that demonstrate momentum levels and anticipate changes. Among these is the *moving average (MA)* of price.

MA is nothing more than the average price over a fixed number of sessions. For example, if you use a 20-day moving average, it consists of the last 20 days added together and then divided by 20. Tomorrow, the oldest day is removed and the newest day added in and the average is recalculated.

Key Point
Moving averages help spot true trends, whereas short-term price patterns may be chaotic and less reliable.

exhaustion gap

A gap occurring at the end of a trend, signifying a loss of momentum and a reversal in price direction.

moving average (MA)

The average price over a fixed number of sessions, adjusted for each new session by removing the oldest and replacing it with the newest day and then dividing the total by the total number of days.

The calculation becomes cumbersome for longer-span MA like the popular 200-day moving average. Fortunately, with online free charting, MA is easily added into charts instantly and without the need to perform any math.

The MA's purpose is to remove the short-term volatility from the price trend and to show how the average price trend is evolving over time. This is most applicable when the MA is below or above current price and remains there as the current trend moves forward, and the trigger for action takes place when price and MA cross over.

To make MA even more applicable, it helps to weight the latest days on the theory that more recent portions of the period are more relevant than the older days. The most popular weighting formula is called *exponential moving average (EMA)*. This is a formula built into online charts to adjust MA to weight the most recent entries.

The most popular MA-based formula is called MACD, which is an abbreviation of *moving average convergence/divergence*. This daunting title simply refers to the analysis of two separate moving average lines, how they relate to price levels, and how the two move closer together or farther apart.

These relationships—breadth between averages and price or between the two averages—help to anticipate a coming price reversal. And as the two lines converge and then cross, or diverge and move farther apart, technicians interpret the changes in terms of how they affect momentum.

Key Point
The trends you spot in changing moving averages give you insight. By the time the lines cross, most traders already know a reversal has taken place, so the smart move is to spot a coming reversal before everyone else acts.

exponential moving average (EMA)

A formula for weighted moving average, used to provide great impact to the latest entries on a stock price chart.

oscillator

Technical indicators that track price movement and identify overbought or oversold conditions. These aid in picking the best entry and exit points in trades.

MA analysis serves as a reliable method of confirming chart patterns or candlestick indicators. Beyond MA, you may use dozens of more advanced indicators. These are broadly called *oscillators*. These are indicators that track trends in order to identify when a stock is either overbought or oversold. When oscillators reach extreme levels on their side, they act as signals. Traders rely on oscillators to find entry and exit points. Following are two of the most widely used. First is the *Chaikin Money Flow (CMF)*. This is an indicator that calculates when buying or selling pressure reaches a point of extreme, and when traders should sell (overbought) or buy (oversold).

The CMF summarizes the *accumulation/distribution line*, which is based on the theory that volume tends to increase before a stock's price moves. So it tracks this trend and identifies positive or negative money flow (volume flow).

A second oscillator is the *Relative Strength Index (RSI)*. This is an analysis of momentum that compares recent upwards and downward movements in the stock and uses averages of up days and down days to calculate a single value showing traders the strength or weakness of price at current levels.

These more technical indicators may involve complex mathematical calculations. Fortunately, you need only understand the concept behind the calculation in order to use it. Online free charting services calculate numerous oscillators for you and add them to charts as additional charting segments or color-coded overlays along with the latest price information.

Key Point

Online free charting has opened up a broad range of complex technical indicators to everyone. However, it is important to understand what is being calculated before making trading decisions based on how those indicators change.

Trading is made more efficient with the Internet, but also more complicated. The volume of information may be counterproductive. For this reason, it makes sense to pick a short list of indicators you believe provide the most reliable initial and confirming information, and track those indicators. If trading direction is uncertain, you can also add in additional indicators if that helps; but start out with fewer rather than with more.

The next chapter expands on observed technical indicators with a discussion of signals and confirmation. Signals point to price changes at which entry or exit are best timed; and confirmation is essential to the reliable application of technical theory.

TO BE CONTINUED...

228

13

SIGNALS AND CONFIRMATION

The decision to open new positions or to close existing ones relies on recognition of specific reversal signals, as a first step. Chapter 10 described entry and exit signals in the context of swing trading. In this chapter, these starting points are expanded to show how they are used along with confirmation indicators, to fine-tune the timing of entry and exit.

Reversal is signaled by patterns in the price trend itself; however, this can be greatly expanded to include well-known candlestick reversal indicators with high reliability. Methods of reversal confirmation are going to be found in both candlestick patterns and well-known technical signals. These include popular patterns that test resistance and support; gapping price action; and momentum oscillators.

Key Point
Reversal does not consist of any one type of indicator. It can be found in many price, volume, and momentum indicators, and confirmation may also consist of a mix of indicator types.

The concept is not advanced, but its application can be elusive. In theory, the process of identifying reversal and then waiting for confirmation makes sense. You are going to find an abundance of reversal signals in charts, as well as confirmation in many forms. However, in the excitement of the moment, traders easily fall prey to a tendency to act impulsively. Remember a few important tips:

1. *Be patient.* Successful traders are known for their patience. There is an old market adage: The market rewards patience. This is true. This means, of course, that if you are compelled to take profits too quickly or get into positions before the positive trend ends, you are not being patient.

2. *Resist the impulse to act too quickly.* As a separate issue from patience, the trader's enemy is impulsiveness. Some traders start out patiently but then give in to impulse. A common symptom among traders is to believe in their own intuition. A good rule of thumb is that intuition is often right, but just as often, it is wrong. In addition, all humans tend to remember the times when intuition was perfectly timed, but to forget the other 50 percent of times when it was flawed. Be aware that intuition can create impulse even among the most patient of traders, but this should be resisted. Trading demands discipline.

3. *Create a methodical trading system and stick with it.* Know what works and what doesn't. Look for signals rather than listening to your gut instincts. Signals are more reliable, even though the human tendency is to believe that gut instinct is reliable. So a system should include awareness of a range of signals, with focus on the most reliable ones, located in the right positions in the current trend, and confirmed independently. Rational observation based on known reversal signals is far more reliable than instinct, intuition, or emotion.

SWING TRADE REVERSALS

The well-known swing trading approach relies on reversal signals, mainly found in three types: the narrow-range day (NRD), also known as a doji in candlestick jargon; the volume spike; and the reversal day.

Key Point

Swing traders are focused on very short-term trends, those lasting three to five days. However, reversal may be delayed far beyond this small window.

These are signals that short-term trends (those extending between three and five days) are about to end. However, even swing traders relying almost exclusively on these realize that they are only the first step. Before acting on the reversal indicators, the signs have to be confirmed.

Examples

Reversing Course: You have entered a position expecting an uptrend. Immediately following, the price rises but after four days you notice momentum has slowed down. As the price levels out, you close the position expecting a short-term reversal. This is a typical swing trade; however, you also understand that both entry and exit would have been more reliable if you had confirmation for each.

Confirmation may come in several forms. These include:

1. *Two or more of the basic signals occurring close together.* The concurrent appearance of two (or even all three) of the swing trading signals is, indeed, strong confirmation that reversal is likely to occur, and quickly.

An example is found in the three-month chart of Chevron (CVX). During November, a reversal day provided a clue that the six-session uptrend might be ending. By itself, the reversal day is not enough, however, even though it also followed a sharp downward price gap. The narrow-range day (NRD) that followed three sessions later made a compelling case for reversal. For those still not sure, the following day was marked by the beginning of a downtrend and a very prominent volume spike. In Figure 13.1, all three of the swing trading reversal signs were present.

Figure 13.1 Reversal Signals—Example 1

Source: Stockcharts.com.

2. *Confirmation from a momentum oscillator.* A second type of confirmation is found in the momentum oscillator. In this variety, you find one or more of the swing trading signals, but also see a change in momentum. For example, in Figure 13.2, the Relative Strength Index (RSI) identifies the speed of change and also marks times when a stock is overbought or oversold In the case of Sears Holding (SHLD), the pre-Christmas price demonstrated both NRDs and a volume spike, and then a strong downward price gap. This could have been a confusing signal given the downward gapping action; however, during this period, RSI also moved below the index point of 30 and remained there for the rest of the charted period. This is an exceptionally strong oversold signal that foreshadowed a price reversal and uptrend. Although not shown on this chart, the SHLD price trend in January did move upward strongly, increasing 20 points to the $50 level.

Figure 13.2 Reversal Signals—Example 2

Source: Stockcharts.com.

3. *Confirmation from well-known technical indicators.* A third source for confirmation is going to be found in traditional technical indicators, notably those testing resistance or support but failing. Look for double tops or bottoms or head and shoulders formation to anticipate reversal; and use those signals as confirmation of candlestick and swing trading signs. Reversal is most likely when price tests resistance during an uptrend, or support during a downtrend. If the signals appear when price is testing these trading range borders, the chances of reversal are far stronger than when the same developments occur at mid-range.

Valuable Resource
A handy cross-reference for many popular technical indicators you can use for confirmation (and arranged by categories) can be found at
www.tradecision.com/support/indicators.htm.

4. *Confirmation in exceptionally strong candlestick indicators.* Candlestick reversal indicators come in dozens of shapes and sizes, as explained in the next section. These provide not only exceptional initial indicators to be independently confirmed, but also provide exceptional confirmation of other signs.

Some candlestick developments work as part of the swing trading signal. For example, the NRD (or doji) and reversal day are both commonly found within candlestick reversal indicators.

Valuable Resource
Many of the most popular and effective candlestick reversals are illustrated and explained at
http://candlestickcourse.com/candlestick-reversal-patterns/.

CANDLESTICK REVERSALS

The vast numbers of candlestick reversal signs make these a part of entry and exit timing. The same rules of reversal apply: There must be a trend to reverse, and it is wise to seek confirmation of the signals (or to accept candlestick reversals as a form of confirmation of other indicators).

Key Point

A reversal can only exist when there is a trend to reverse. As obvious as this seems, it is easily overlooked by candlestick analysts.

Among the most reliable of reversal signals are the white soldiers, black crows, and engulfing patterns. The appearance of long shadows also serves as a very promising signal that the trend is likely to turn and move in the opposite direction.

White soldiers is a set of three or more consecutive sessions. All three are white (upward moving). Each session opens within the range of the previous session's real body, and then closes higher, as shown in Figure 13.3.

Figure 13.3 White Soldiers

Source: Stockcharts.com.

The chart for IBM began with a clear example of white soldiers after a downtrend. This introduced an uptrend that then paused before resuming. It is also noteworthy that the opening price of the third white soldiers session established a new support level for the stock.

Figure 13.4 Black Crows
Source: Stockcharts.com.

White soldiers is 82 percent reliable, based on a study performed by Thomas Bulkowski.[1] Another highly reliable pattern is the opposite of white soldiers, black crows, as shown in Figure 13.4. This consists of three or more sessions, each opening within the range of the previous real body and then closing lower. This pattern leads to reversal 78 percent of the times it appears. For example, the three-month chart of SPDR Gold Trust (GLD) includes an 18-point uptrend that concludes at the top with an example of black crows. The indicator is confirmed a couple of sessions later with consecutive doji (NRD) sessions. After this turning point, the price declines 24 points by the end of the charted period. Although the black crows of the GLD chart contain relatively small-range sessions, its signal was reliable and important in timing for this security.

[1] Thomas Bulkowski, *Encyclopedia of Candlestick Charts* (Hoboken, NJ: John Wiley & Sons, 2008).

Both white soldiers and black crows appear often enough that you are likely to find them in your charting experience. The high reliability makes them important enough to get your attention.

Key Point
Just because a particular candlestick indicator leads to reversal most of the time, you cannot rely on them alone. You also need independent confirmation.

The engulfing pattern consists of two sessions of opposite colors. The second session extends both higher and lower than the first. In the bullish version, the first session is black and the second session is white. It opens lower than the previous close and then moves to close higher than the previous open. The greater range plus the extension on both sides beyond the range, make the engulfing pattern a powerful signal. However, in the bullish variety, it leads to reversal only 63 percent of the time—still better than 50–50, but not as strong as many other indicators.

An example is found in Figure 13.5. Target (TGT) had a very strong uptrend that began with a bullish engulfing pattern. The large upside gap and volume spike confirmed the reversal.

Figure 13.5 Bullish Engulfing Pattern
Source: Stockcharts.com.

The bearish version is more reliable and leads to reversal 79 percent of the times it's found. That is highly reliable. It consists of a white session followed by a black one. The black session opens higher than the previous session's close, and then moves down to close lower. Like its bullish cousin, the bearish engulfing pattern does not look like much, but the contrast between the two sessions demonstrates a shift between buyers and sellers.

An example is seen in Figure 13.6, the chart of KB Home (KBH). After a three-month period of modestly strong support, the price turns and moves downward.

Figure 13.6 Bearish Engulfing Pattern

Source: Stockcharts.com.

In the month following this period, the price did return to the upside, so the engulfing pattern could be interpreted in one of two ways. Either it accurately predicted a short-term downtrend, or failed given the eventual price rise in the month of January.

Key Point

Some indicators can be interpreted as either successful or a failure, depending on how long a period you observe. If your window is very short-term in duration, the conclusion you reach could be opposite that of an analyst looking further into the future.

A final reversal indicator worth observing is the long shadow. This is the extension of a day's trading, either above or below the open-close range. In a session at or near the top of an uptrend, an unusually long upper shadow is a sign of declining momentum among buyers. The inability to drive price higher and close at those levels reveals that the trend is turning. By the same argument, a long lower shadow in a session after a downtrend reveals the same decline in momentum among sellers.

For example, in Figure 13.7, Verizon (VZ) exhibited a moderate uptrend, but note the extremely long lower shadow came right before a three-week downtrend. After this occurred, prices rebounded and moved higher, but it is impossible to ignore the size of the lower shadow relative to trading in the period before it appeared.

Figure 13.7 Long Shadow Example

Source: Stockcharts.com.

Confirmation is found in the hanging man of the session itself (a small real body with a long lower shadow), and then by the two doji sessions appearing a couple of days later. These further exhibited the struggle between buyer and seller and the exhaustion hinted at by the long lower shadow. Then the price dropped.

Interpreting what candlestick indicators reveal is not difficult, assuming that the required confirmation signals also show up. Making this more difficult, short-term trends often are very short-term in nature. Swing traders seek trends lasting between three and five sessions and other traders may expect to see trends last only two to three weeks at the most. It is all relative, however. In swing trading terms, a three-week trend is quite lengthy, but for more conservative investing purposes, anything under a month has to be considered unreliable. The short-term trends are good for approximately entry and exit in a high-volume trading strategy. This is where candlesticks provide the greatest value.

SIGNAL FAILURE

A final note has to be made concerning the possibility of signal failure. No indicators are ever going to be 100 percent reliable. Even highly reliable candlesticks confirmed by other price indicators, volume spikes, momentum oscillators and failed tests of resistance and support are going to fail some of the time. The key about creating a methodical system for reversal indicators and confirmation is to improve the percentage of times your trading decisions are timed well.

Key Point
You cannot avoid failure of even the most strongly confirmed indicators. The best you can expect is to improve your percentages by applying the basic principle: Find a reversal and confirm it before you enter a trade.

You are going to find plenty of examples of signal failure if you look for them. One example was found in the chart of Toyota Motors (TM). In September, the highlighted two-session developed represented a bearish separating lines signal. From this, you would expect prices to fall. However, not only did prices rise, they exhibited a strong runaway gapping pattern, a strongly bullish development.

Figure 13.8 Signal Failure—Example 1

Source: Stockcharts.com.

An even stronger example of signal failure was found in the chart of Alcoa (AA). This included three separate bearish signals, which is a lot of confirmation in a small amount of time. First was a bearish thrusting line, followed by a strong bearish piercing line, and then a volume spike. In spite of all the evidence pointing to downward price movement, prices rose strongly before finally retreating.

Figure 13.9 Signal Failure—Example 2

Source: Stockcharts.com.

In the short term, the bearish signals failed. A contrary interpretation is that the signals were accurate but reaction was delayed. This points out how elusive charting can be, even with strong signals. In this case, you can interpret matters in two different ways and both are supportable. If you rely on very short-term trends, the signal failed. But if you are seeking verification for longer-term trends, then the strong bearish indicators were reliable and accurate.

Key Point

Every signal can fail, even the signal that is confirmed by one or two other signals. There are no guarantees; but relying on strong signals and confirmation does improve the timing of entry and exit.

This brings up the importance of how long a period you expect trends to last. Swing traders are focused on very short-term trends, but many technical analysts and chartists take a longer point of view. The next chapter explains this by going through the Dow Theory and showing how its precepts relate to various trends.

TO BE CONTINUED...

14

TECHNICAL ANALYSIS, DOW THEORY, AND PRACTICE

The basis for technical analysis is found in a few principles and theories that deal with price behavior. In other words, prices move for specific reasons, some beyond the economic observations of supply and demand. So beyond the economic reasons for price movement, some ideas have been offered to explain price movement as either efficient or random.

An analysis of market behavior demonstrates, however, that price movement is neither efficient nor random. It is inefficient in the short term primarily because prices tend to overreact to all current and new information and then to correct later. For example, when earnings exceed expectations, right after the announcement is made the stock price might move way ahead of what seems justified. In the following session or two, the surge is corrected and prices retreat. This is not efficient.

Key Point
Contrary to popular theories, the stock market is neither efficient nor random. It is a risky venture to buy and sell shares of stock due to the unknown forces that drive prices upward or downward.

Prices cannot be justified as random, either. If prices were random, the cause and effect of news and price movement would not be consistent by any measure. However, when good news is released, prices tend to rise; and when bad news is released, prices tend to fall. Furthermore, prices overall tend to follow market averages. So when there is a big price surge or a big price drop, a majority of listed stocks tend to move in the same direction as the big index stocks. This is not random; in fact, it is highly predictable.

THE EFFICIENT MARKET

The first interesting theory about price behavior is called the *efficient market theory (EMT)*. This theory states simply that prices react to changes in the company, in the market as a whole, and in the economy; and that the current price of stock has already been adjusted for all known information about that company.

The EMT is cynical because it concludes that analyzing a company's financial reports or studying stock charts is meaningless. Since all prices are fair and efficient because the *smart* investors have already bid prices to their proper levels, there is never a discrepancy between price and value.

Key Point
The efficient market theory cynically states that you cannot make informed selections based on analysis; most investors and traders instinctively know that analysis is the key to profits.

EMT is controversial and it has many proponents. However, it is flawed for at least three reasons:

1. *There are no consistently* smart *investors*. In spite of what the academic theory claims, there are no smart investors out there, at least not enough of them. Truthfully, no investors are consistently able to produce profits by their analysis and decisions. If they were, then the efficient market theory might make sense.

2. *Short-term price movement is demonstrably inefficient.* When you study the cause and effect between news about a company and its stock price behavior, you immediately realize that volatility is more important than news and information. Perhaps actual economic and financial news should be more important, but the simple truth is that prices behave irrationally. An alternative, the inefficient market theory, makes more sense. EMT is really nothing more than wishful thinking. In a perfect world, the markets—like everything else—would be rational, behave predictably, and make sense. But the truly interesting thing about investing or trading in the market is its volatility and unpredictability.

3. *Short-term fads and trends contradict the tidy theory behind EMT.* If you look back over the history of the stock market, you realize that the driving forces behind big price movements have often been irrational, short-lived, and highly inefficient. For example, the well-known dot-com bubble between 1995 and 2000 was characterized by rapid growth in the value of Internet stocks, followed by an equally rapid price decline. Why? The trend was driven largely by speculation but with no tangible support. The price growth grew from a belief that companies could grow based on future product or service development even though they currently had nothing of value to offer. Initial public offerings were made for companies that did not even have products. The speculative craze ended very suddenly (and inefficiently) in 2000, once the speculative phase was exhausted.

Figure 14.1 shows how the NASDAQ Composite fell in the three years off the dot-com high. It took that long for the index to begin an upward climb, back to about the 2,400 level by mid-2010. NASDAQ is the exchange on which most IT stocks are listed and was the major exchange hit by the dot-com decline.

Key Point

Fads like the dot-com bubble prove that markets are anything but efficient; they are more prone to emotional and irrational exuberance.

The dot-com occurrence is only a recent example of how markets operate inefficiently. The dot-com craze was irrational because a majority of the Internet companies had no products to bring to the market, and as a result had never reported profits, or even revenues. The entire matter was one of perception about future value. A few well-known companies (like Google, eBay, and Amazon.com) did survive and moved forward to become very successful examples of Internet-based companies. But the relatively small number out of hundreds of dot-com companies makes the point that markets are driven more by enthusiastic perceptions than by actual numbers.

EMT is supported and believed largely in academic circles, and much less among actual investors. Academic theories are comforting and reliable, but they remain only theories. No one who has invested capital in the volatile markets of recent years is likely to believe in efficiency as an attribute of the stock market. Actually, being a proponent of EMT is more a matter of faith than of proof. Some observers want the market to be efficient, and so they believe in EMT, even when the evidence shows how inefficient the market truly is. Or, as the successful contrarian Warren Buffett has explained it, "Apparently, a reluctance to recant, and thereby to demystify the priesthood, is not limited to theologians."[1]

---

[1] Warren Buffett, Chairman's Letter to Shareholders, February 28, 1989.

Figure 14.1 The Dot-Com Decline
Source: Nasdaq.

THE RANDOM WALK

While EMT suggests that stock is always efficiently priced (and therefore you cannot outperform the market except as a consequence of luck), another theory suggests that price behavior is never based on anything predictable, but is completely random.

The *random walk theory* is the belief that price behavior cannot be predicted because it does not act on any predictive fundamental or technical indicators. Under the random walk theory, there is an equal chance that a stock's price will either rise or fall from current levels.

The random walk theory contradicts the widely accepted beliefs by both fundamental and technical analysts. Under the theory of fundamental analysis, the long-term value of a company is based on competitive strength, profitability, revenue and market expansion, working capital controls, and capitalization. Under the theory of technical analysis, price is predictable based on chart patterns, momentum indicators, and reversal signals such as those found in candlesticks.

Examples

Not So Random: You have owned stock in a company for several years and you notice a clear relationship between earnings reports and stock prices. Although the price rises and falls with market direction in the short term, when earnings are better than expected, the stock price builds higher trading range levels; and in two of the past five years, earnings were lower than expected and the price levels fell. This is a predictable cause and effect that you have observed, meaning that for this company, price movement is anything but random.

Neither fundamental nor technical analysis provides 100 percent certainty of profitable decisions or of well-timed entry and exit from positions. However, the analytical tools are intended to improve the timing of decisions, especially for traders relying on a range of technical patterns.

The random walk denies the reliability of any fundamental or technical analysis. It is at least as cynical as the efficient market theory and just as misleading. While short-term markets are clearly chaotic and inefficient, both short-term and long-term pricing can be tied to both fundamental and technical trends. In fact, far from being random, a more supportable belief about price behavior is that fundamental and technical indicators confirm one another, even though the timing is different. In other words, short-term price strength is derived from solid long-term financial strength, and long-term fundamental trends are reflected in the stock's long-term pricing trends as well.

The random walk theory is supported for the most part by academics and some economists—mostly those who rely more on theoretical application and mathematical models and less on a study of how invested positions gain or lose value in the real world of the stock market. Those who subscribe to the random walk theory rationalize that prices have to be random because the market is efficient and prices in all currently known facts and influences at each moment. This is illogical, and you can prove this by simply observing the correlation between several forces: earnings news and prices; economic news and economic effects of companies (unemployment, inflation, interest rates, etc.); and changes in sector positions or cyclical movement based on economic change, to name a few.

The theory persists based on academic studies in spite of many developments in analysis, notably free online charting and instant price analysis as a result of the free charting and mathematical tools. The theory has been around for a long time, first introduced in an academic paper by British statistician Maurice Kendall (1953, *The Analytics of Economic Time Series, Part I: Prices*). Two important books expanded on the idea. The first was *The Random Character of Stock Market Prices* (1964) by Professor Paul Cootner. The theory was then expanded upon by Professor Burton Malkiel in *A Random Walk Down Wall Street* (1973).

Key Point
The flaw in the *proof* of the random walk theory is that price behavior in the market is not the same as a statistical concept. There is a true cause and effect in the market.

These papers and books were well written and thoughtful, but they were based on theory and not on practice. Most investors and traders are better served by relying on fundamental and technical analysis, not so much to ensure profits and eliminate losses, but to improve the ratio between profits and losses based on a rational and serious study of a company's strength and future profit potential (fundamental) and on the strength of the current price as it trends upward or downward (technical).

Some efforts have been undertaken to prove the random walk theory by statistical methods. A hypothetical stock's price is predicted based on coin flips, for example, when you know that there is an equal chance of the result being heads or tails. When a series of random coin flips is charted and described as "past performance," proponents of the random walk claim that the pattern can be used to predict future outcomes of coin flipping.

Examples

Disapproving Proof: There are many systems and methods for judging a company's performance based on its stock price. Tracking dividend achievers (companies whose dividend has increased every year for at least 10 years) demonstrates that this classification of companies tends as a group to outperform the market averages. Because many companies fall into this group, it is a large enough sample to provide compelling evidence challenging the random walk theory.

While the random events like coin flips will produce patterns, and those patterns can be interpreted as predictive tools, there is an important distinction between coin and stock prices. We know that the coin flip is random and that all future coin flips are going to be random as well. However, in studying stock price behavior of a company with a known history of a specific volatility level, existing within a specific market sector and with a known competitive position, these known factors certainly affect price movement.

For example, a company with a strong dividend yield, low debt ratio, and consistent record of profits is likely to continue to experience rising prices over time. (If you doubt this, check the 10-year history of Wal-Mart or any other successful and well-managed company that dominates its sector). The reality of the factors influencing stock prices makes the coin flip exercise a statistically inapplicable comparison.

A problem in applying statistical modeling to stock prices, especially to prove the random walk theory, is that coins are not going to behave like stocks. Just because coin flips or any other non-stock price events appear to be random does not mean that stock prices must also be random. Stock price behavior is not random, but is directly influenced by market volatility, financial news, investor and trader perceptions, and dozens of supply-and-demand realities. Just because a stock's price is difficult to predict does not mean it is also random.

The random walk theory conveniently ignores both price trends and momentum. The basic tenet of technical analysis relies on the observed fact that observation of past trends (price direction, momentum, volatility, duration of short-term trends, and more) can be used to predict future price movement. In fact, studies by many market experts provide a strong case to prove that price behavior is not random. Among these tests, a 10-year study by Martin Weber, a behavioral finance researcher, tracked market price changes. Weber found specific patterns that made long-term pricing trends predictable. For example, he found that stocks with upward price patterns and increased earnings tended to outperform other stocks for the following six months.

Key Point

The problem with the random walk theory is that it ignores the easily observed trends and momentum factors that do directly affect price movement.

Another challenge to the random walk theory was published by Professors Andrew W. Lo and Archie Craig MacKinley (1999, *A Non-Random Walk Down Wall Street*). In this book, a series of tests demonstrated that at least some degree of predictability is present in stocks based on a comparison between price behavior and other influences (earnings, for example). The same authors wrote a paper (2005, "The Adaptive Market Hypothesis") in which financial activity (price behavior) is influenced not randomly, but by the same factors affecting evolution (competition, adaptation, and natural selection).

This is an intriguing concept, because all of these evolutionary concepts also affect a company's ability to survive. Failure to compete (due to obsolete products or better-capitalized competitors), failure to adapt (developing new products as new technology or markets emerge), or the forces of natural selection (the market's preference for one company over another due to any number of reasons) are all interesting. These describe what happens to species in nature as well as to companies in the market.

One of the authors of this book, Lo, explained this: "Prices reflect as much information as dictated by the combination of environmental conditions and the number of 'species' in the economy." [2]

Within any cyclical period, a stock's price movement can appear very random; this does not prove that all prices act randomly at all times. The environmental model makes this point. If a number of animals in one isolated region starve to death and die out because there is no food, it does not prove that a species goes extinct by random selection. Other animals of the same species are likely to thrive elsewhere and even when one species does go extinct, there are usually logical reasons. Some may be hunted into extinction, while others fail to adapt to their environment or run up against the introduction of new competing species. Some may die out for no apparent logical reason, which also fails to prove that evolution is random.

[2] Andrew W. Lo and Craig MacKinley, "The Adaptive Market Hypothesis," *Journal of Investment Consulting 7*, no. 2 (2005), pp.21 - 44.

CHARLES DOW AND HIS MARKET THEORY

Charles Dow (1851–1902) wrote a series of editorials in his financial publication, *The Customer's Afternoon Letter*, a two-page summary of each day's financial news that in 1889 was renamed the *Wall Street Journal*. Dow had met his future business partner Edward Jones while the two worked together on the *Providence Evening Press* in Rhode Island. The two men also devised an index they called the Dow Jones Stock Average, which consisted of 11 companies (nine railroads, one steamship company, and Western Union).

In 1896, Dow created a new index of 12 stocks. He added their prices together and divided by 12 to arrive at a simple price average. Today, index averaging is normally done in two ways. A *price-weighted average* like the best-known one, the *Dow Jones Industrial Average (DJIA)*, consists of 30 industrial companies' stocks. In this kind of averaging method, higher-priced stocks have greater influence on the index than lower-priced stocks.

price-weighted average

A kind of stock market average in which the prices of components are added together and divided by the number of stocks used; the result is that higher-priced stocks have more influence on the average than lower-priced stocks.

Valuable Resource
A very interesting article about the Dow theory and its evolution is found at marketthoughts.com:
www.marketthoughts.com/dow_theory.html.

Dow Jones Industrial Average (DJIA)

A price-weighted average of 30 blue-chip industrial stocks, popularly used to judge the trend and strength or weakness of the stock market.

capitalization-weighted average

A stock market average in which components are weighted according to their market capitalization rather than by price per share.

In the case of the DJIA, as of June 1, 2010, four companies—IBM, 3M, Chevron, and McDonalds—account for more than one-fourth of the total index value of the DJIA.[3]

The second method of developing an index is called the *capitalization-weighted average*. The best known of these are the S&P 500 and the NASDAQ Composite. Under this method, the components of the index are weighted according to the size of their total capitalization. In these averages, large price movement in higher-capitalization companies has greater influence on the index value than price movement in components with less capitalization.

Charles Dow did not develop his index theory all at once. Originally, his idea was to develop a method for tracking business trends such as earnings, as well as price trends based on price behavior among leading stocks. This concept was later given a name, the *Dow Theory*. Charles Dow himself never used this term, which was formalized after his death. Dow noticed that stock prices tended to move along with other, broader business trends like growth of the economy, for example. He identified business cycles as important influences on price behavior.

The first person to use the term *Dow Theory* was S. A. Nelson in his 1903 book, *The ABC of Stock Speculation*.

[3]IBM = 9.37 percent; 3M = 5.89 percent; Chevron = 5.45 percent; and McDonalds = 5.00 percent. *Source*: The Dow Jones Companies, June 1, 2010.

Key Point
The Dow Theory provides a framework for identifying and quantifying market-wide trends.

There are six specific tenets that make up the Dow Theory as developed by William P. Hamilton, fourth editor of the *Wall Street Journal*, who actually developed and refined the theory:

1. *Markets consist of three levels of price movement, or trends.* Price behavior consists of a *primary trend*, a period when the direction—upward or downward—is clearly established and lasts between several months and several years. The *secondary trend* is a movement in the direction opposite the primary trend, in which price levels retrace the primary movement between 33 percent and 66 percent, and which lasts from a few days to a few months. The *minor trend* is the movement of only a few days, which may move in either direction.

2. *Trends all contain three specific stages.* Every trend is made up of three distinct parts. These are predictable and exact. First is the *accumulation phase*, a period in which contrarian and experienced investors and traders buy shares (during an up-trend) or sell shares (during a downtrend). This often occurs when overall market sentiment is to do the opposite. Second is the *public participation phase*, a period in which the market follows the early lead introduced during the accumulation phase, and buying or selling becomes widespread. Third is the *distribution phase*, the period in which those who led accumulation now sell appreciated shares or buy depressed shares, marking the last portion of the trend.

3. *All news is discounted.* This rule tells you that the market absorbs information, which goes into changing the price. Some price changes occur even before the news is announced, in anticipation of that news. The discounting of news and information is also called efficiency, and this rule has been used as a rationalization of the efficient market theory.

primary trend

The overall direction of the market, either bullish or bearish, which lasts from a few months to several years.

secondary trend

A trend lasting from a few days to a few months, with prices moving counter to the direction of the primary trend.

minor trend

A price trend of only a few days, moving either upward or downward.

4. *Market averages have to confirm one another before a new trend can be identified.* The original theory was based on the importance of the *rails* (later changed to be called *transportation* and to encompass trucking, shipping, and airlines). In the time of Charles Dow, the United States was expanding quickly as an industrial power, and factories needed to ship goods from widely dispersed areas into urban centers. This led to the conclusion that the strength or weakness of the transportation sector dictated the existence or change in a primary trend. Under this rule, today's Dow Theory is based on confirmation between averages. When one average begins moving, it does not represent a new trend until a second average also changes direction, confirming the new trend. For primary trends, the industrial and transportation averages are the most important indicators of trends and changes in trends. Today, the transportation sector continues to offer symptoms of economic health within the economy. The more production and selling, the more goods are moved to markets. So the transportation average is a crucial confirmation tool for industrial trends.

5. *Trends in price must be confirmed further by changes in volume of trading.* Dow Theory observers have noted that changes in prices and trends that occur on low volume might be false indicators, or are caused by deceptive actions such as *short covering*. But when price direction changes and volume are also higher than average, this is seen as additional confirmation that the trend is legitimate.

6. *Trends continue in effect until signals establish a clear reversal.* Trends do not simply evaporate or stop without a signal developing to show that something has taken place, often a reversal and the beginning of a new trend in the opposite direction. Short-term price movement is always chaotic, and for this reason Dow Theory observers rely on strong reversal signals, changes in volume, and other technical tools.

The Dow Theory is not perfect, but it does provide a framework for managing short-term market chaos and identifying longer-term trends. The Dow Theory employs averages, meaning everything is discounted;

accumulation phase

The first phase of a trend, during which contrarians and experienced investors and traders buy (in an uptrend) or sell (in a downtrend).

public participation phase

The second phase of a trend, in which the market follows the lead of those in the accumulation phase and buys or sells shares in the indicated direction.

with this in mind, the indicators are not perfect and everything has to be confirmed.

Key Point

All indicated reversals located using the Dow Theory rely specifically on confirmation. This is a requirement before a new trend can be called.

Is the Dow Theory still valid today? With the Internet making market news and information widely and easily accessible, some critics have stated that the Dow Theory is outdated. However, especially for traders who rely on confirmation as a basic tool for timing of entry and exit, the rules governing the Dow Theory apply even in the completely automated age.

In all forms of analysis, both fundamental and technical, the purpose is to improve your selection judgment, timing, and knowledge. No one has a system to ensure 100 percent success or perfect entry and exit timing. The stock market provides one of the most promising aspects of the free enterprise system by allowing everyone, even those with modest levels of capital to invest, with a place to start.

distribution phase

The third stage in a trend, in which leading investors or traders sell appreciated shares (uptrend) or buy depressed shares (downtrend), marking the end of the trend.

short covering

Buying activity resulting from holders of shorted stock closing positions; when short covering occurs at a high volume, it may create an artificially high buy indicator.

THE END!

12b-1 fee
A fee charged by a mutual fund for marketing and promotion to attract new investors.

accumulated depreciation
The sum of all years' depreciation expense recorded and claimed. The annual expense is offset by the accumulation account, which is a negative asset, or a reduction of the book value of capital assets.

accumulation phase
The first phase of a trend, during which contrarians and experienced investors and traders buy (in an uptrend) or sell (in a downtrend).

accumulation/distribution line
An analysis of volume in relation to price, based on the CMF theory and stating that volume trends precede price movement.

amortization
The yearly amount of expense recorded and offset by a reduction to a prepaid asset account. For example, when a 36-month insurance premium is prepaid, it is amortized over the 36 months rather than reported as expense in the year paid.

annual report
A financial and marketing summary issued by corporations, including financial statements and detailed explanations, and management's interpretation of its financial and competitive position in the market.

ascending triangle
A pattern of narrowing breadth in the trading range, consisting of flat resistance and rising support, and preceding a likely reversal and downtrend.at the money

at the money
The status of an option when its strike is equal to the current value of the underlying stock.

back-end sales load
A variation of sales commission in a mutual fund, in which the commission is deducted when shares are redeemed rather than when investments are made.

balance sheet
A financial statement reporting the balances of all asset, liability, and net worthy accounts as of the last day of the reporting period.

balanced funds
Mutual funds combining growth and income positions based on positions in stocks or combinations of stocks and bonds.

basket of stocks
The pre-identified, fixed portfolio in the exchange-traded fund (ETF).

bear markets
Markets of declining price trends over a period of months or years.

blue chip
Companies with strong earnings, a history of regular dividend payments, and little or no long-term liabilities; a financially strong and stable company.

book value
The true value of a company based on balance sheet reporting; it is the total of all assets minus the total of all liabilities. When the net value is divided by outstanding shares, the result is book value per share.

breadth
The span of price movement within the current trading range, representing the number of points of movement over time.

breakaway gap
A type of gap that moves prices above or below the trading range and either begins a rally or retreats to the previous level in subsequent sessions.

break-even rate
The rate of return needed from investing activity to absorb inflation and taxes, in order to maintain the purchasing power of investment capital.

breakout
Price movement below support or above resistance, signifying creation of a new trading range or a failed attempt in which prices retreat back to the established trading range.

bull markets
Markets characterized by generally rising prices of stocks over a period of months or years.

buy and hold
An investment strategy involving identification of value investments and purchase of shares, with the intention of holding those shares for the long term.

buy to open/sell to open
The type of opening order being placed. A buy to open is used to create a long position, and a sell to open creates a short position.

calendar spreads
Alternative name for horizontal spreads.

call
An option providing its owner the right but not the obligation to buy 100 shares of a specified stock, at a fixed price, on or before a specified expiration date.

candlesticks
Chart entries based on rectangular boxes that show at a glance the opening and closing price, trading range, and direction of price movement for a trading session.

capital assets
All assets set up to be periodically depreciated because their value outlasts a single accounting year; when fully depreciated, the capital asset's book value is zero.

capital gains
Profits on investments such as stocks, taxed at a lower rate than other income if the asset is owned for one year or more.

capitalization-based funds
Mutual funds specializing in portfolios of companies based on market capitalization (large-cap, mid-cap, or small-cap).

capitalization-weighted average
A stock market average in which components are weighted according to their market capitalization rather than by price per share.

Chaikin Money Flow (CMF)
An oscillator that identifies overbought or oversold conditions through a mathematical analysis of price trends.

channel
Trading within the bounds of resistance and support, which does not break through on either side.

chartist
A trader who studies price patterns through a series of stock charts, looking for early signs for emerging entry or exit points based on how price and volume behave, and using a range of possible technical indicators to make those decisions.

circuit breaker
An automatic halt to trading in all listed securities on exchanges, triggered by exceptionally large price declines and set to last a specified number of hours or until the end of trading for the session.

closed-end fund
A mutual fund with a maximum number of shares outstanding that trades over a stock exchange rather than directly between fund management and investors. Market value of shares rises or falls based on demand and performance rather than on the market value of the portfolio.

closing order
An order placed with a broker to close a position, whether it had been opened long or short.

common gap
A price gap occurring as a part of normal trading activity and without any signal value for changes in the existing trend.

common stock
(called *ordinary shares* in the UK) Ownership in a corporation including voting rights for membership on boards of directors and corporate policies. Common stockholders have the lowest priority in the event of liquidation, below bondholders and preferred stockholders.

compound interest
Interest calculated at a periodic rate based on the stated annual rate. For example, a 4 percent interest rate compounded quarterly represents compound annual interest of 4.06 percent: $(1.01 \times 1.01 \times 1.01 \times 1.01) = 1.0406$, or 4.06 percent.

conduit investment
Any organization that passes through profits to its investors and manages a collective portfolio. The best-known conduit investment is the mutual fund.

confirmation
The use of one indicator to bolster or support the conclusions reached by what a different indicator reveals.

congestion
A price pattern of sideways movement within a narrow trading range, with neither buyers nor sellers in control.

consolidation
A period of indecision in the market, during which neither buyers nor sellers are in command. No one can determine whether prices will be driven higher or lower, so there is little or no movement during this time.

contingent deferred sales load (CDSL)
A back-end load, or sales commission assessed by mutual funds only if shares are redeemed before a specified number of years.

continuation day
A single day with a candlestick pattern providing a sign of a continuation in the trend rather than reversal, due to its position and direction within the trend.

contrarian
An investor or trader who makes decisions based on analysis rather than simply following the majority and who recognizes that the majority is wrong more often than right, so making the opposite decision often is the smart move.

convergence theory
A theory that crowd behavior is created by individuals who bring ideas to the crowd, rather than as a spontaneous matter. In the market, individuals who act in a particular way may influence others to follow their behavior.

convergence/divergence
In technical analysis, the pattern revealed in two moving averages of different numbers of sessions. As the lines move closer together (converge) or farther apart (diverge) the chartist draws conclusions about the coming price direction.

core earnings
A calculated adjustment to net earnings to isolate earnings from the company's primary, or core business. All noncore, nonrecurring, or extraordinary items are adjusted out of the calculation of net earnings allowed under the accounting rules.

cost of goods sold
Expenditures for merchandise, direct labor, freight, and the changes in inventory levels, all attributable directly to generation of revenue.

covered call
A short call opened when the trader also owns 100 shares of the underlying stock. In the event of exercise, the shares are called away at the strike.

cum dividend
Meaning "with dividend," reference to the status of a stockholder entitled to receive a dividend in the current quarter.

current assets
All assets in liquid form, meaning cash or convertible to cash within 12 months.

current liabilities
All debts payable within 12 months, including the current portion of long-term liabilities.

current ratio
A popular test of working capital. Current assets are divided by current liabilities, and the answer is expressed as a single digit.

cycle
An economic tendency for sales volume and profits to change predictably due to economic or calendar timing. Among the best-known of market cycles is that experienced in the retail trade, which goes through specific seasons of high and low sales volume based on consumer buying habits.

day trading
Activity in which positions are entered and exited on the same day so that no open positions remain by the end of the day.

debt ratio
An indicator derived by dividing long-term debt by total capitalization.

deferred assets
Expense payments made in one year but belonging completely to a future year, left as an asset until reversed and transferred in the proper accounting period.

deferred credits
Accounts in the liability section of the balance sheet, representing revenues received but not earned until a future period.

descending triangle
A bullish sign involving flat support and declining resistance. As the breadth shrinks to a very narrow point, the expectation is for a reversal and uptrend to follow.

diagonal spreads
Spreads opened with options on the same underlying stock with different strike prices and different expiration months.

disruption risk
The risk that trading in stocks may be disrupted by political or economic causes, acts of war, or natural disasters.

distribution phase
The third stage in a trend, in which leading investors or traders sell appreciated shares (uptrend) or buy depressed shares (downtrend), marking the end of the trend.

diversification
Spreading of risk among several dissimilar stocks or other investments in order to avoid having a single risk event negatively affect the entire portfolio.

dividend achievers
Companies that have declared and paid dividends without missing a payment for 10 years or more, and that have increased the dividend per share every year.

dividend reinvestment plans (DRIPS)
Features provided to investors when shares of stock are bought, allowing the choice to receive dividends in the form of additional partial shares instead of cash.

dividend yield
The return on dividends paid. To compute the annual dividend yield, divide annual dividends per share by the current price per share; the result is expressed as a percentage.

dogs of the Dow
A measurement of dividend yield and stock prices, based on the belief that the 10 DJIA stocks with the highest dividends relative to stock price are also likely to outperform the market average.

doji
A candlestick with little or no distance between opening and closing, so that a horizontal line is found instead of a rectangle.

dollar cost averaging (DCA)
A system of investing the same dollar amount into the market periodically regardless of price changes over time, on the theory that this reduces risk.

double bottom
A technical pattern consisting of two downward price spikes testing support. The failure to break through precedes a reversal and an uptrend after the double attempt.

double top
A technical pattern in which price rises to the resistance level twice without breaking through permanently; after this, prices are expected to decline.

Dow Jones Industrial Average (DJIA)
A price-weighted average of 30 blue-chip industrial stocks, popularly used to judge the trend and strength or weakness of the stock market.

Dow Theory
A belief in trends set within the markets, based on the original beliefs and observations expressed by Charles Dow.

downtrend
In swing trading, a series of consecutive sessions with lower high prices and lower low prices in each session, compared to the previous session.

dragonfly doji
A bullish doji with a lower shadow only, recognizable by its formation of a capital letter T.

earnings per share (EPS)
The latest reported earnings, expressed as a division of earnings by the total shares outstanding during the reported year.

Eastern technical indicators
The analysis of charts to find price patterns and improve entry and exit of positions, based on the patterns revealed by candlesticks.

effective tax rate
The rate of taxes assessed on taxable income, combining both federal and state rates.

efficient market theory (EMT)
A belief that the price of stock reflects all known information about the company at all times, and changes rationally based on new information as it becomes available.

engulfing pattern
A two-session candlestick formation with the second day longer on both sides of the first day (engulfing its range). A bullish version consists of a black set-up day and a white second day; a bearish version consists of a white set-up day and a black second day.

enterprise value (EV)
An alternative to the measurement of value based on equity alone, or market cap; EV includes all sources of capitalization, including holders of notes and bonds (debtors), as well as common and preferred stockholders.

entry and exit signals
Indicators consisting of price patterns or changes, which traders use to improve the time of buy and sell decisions. These signals are meant to improve their chances of accurate timing to increase profits and reduce losses.

equity funds
Mutual funds that create a portfolio from investments in stocks (equities) of listed companies.

exchange-traded fund (ETF)
A type of mutual fund with a pre identified basket of stocks with a common element. The ETF is traded over public exchanges just like shares of stock.

ex-dividend date
The cut-off date for earning of dividends. Stockholders who own stock before ex-date earn a dividend to be paid a few weeks later. Anyone buying stock on or after the ex-date has to wait until the next quarter before earning dividends.

exercise
The act by an owner of a call to buy shares at the fixed strike price, or by the owner of a put to sell shares at the fixed strike price.

exhaustion gap
A gap occurring at the end of a trend, signifying a loss of momentum and a reversal in price direction.

exit and entry signals
Indicators consisting of price patterns or changes, which traders use to improve the timing of buy and sell decisions. These signals are meant to improve their chances of accurate timing to increase profits and reduce losses.

expiration date
The date when an option becomes worthless; the Saturday following the third Friday of the specified expiration month.

exponential moving average (EMA)
A formula for weighted moving average, used to provide great impact to the latest entries on a stock price chart.

extreme reaction risk
The risk that timing of buying or selling decisions will be based on overreaction to market conditions rather than made rationally or based on observed technical signals.

extrinsic value
The portion of an option's premium beyond both intrinsic value and time value, reflecting the implied volatility of the option and varying based on time to expiration and proximity between current value of stock and strike price of the option. The price volatility of the underlying stock also directly impacts the extrinsic value of the option.

failed signal
A technical signal indicating a price direction about to emerge (most notably a price reversal) that does not materialize or is contradicted in actual price movement.

fair value
A fundamental indicator intended to value a stock and its growth potential based on a specific measurement; this is compared to the current market value of stock to seek bargain prices.

family of funds
A group of funds offered by one mutual fund company but with different investment objectives.

financial ratios
Tests of related financial data including operating results for a period of time (usually one full year), or the working capital and capitalization status as of a specified date (usually year-end).

financial statements
Summaries of a company's operations for a defined period of time (one year or the latest quarter), and of the values of assets, liabilities, and equity accounts as of a specific date.

fiscal year
The tax year used by a corporation, which may end in any quarter selected by the company. Fiscal years may correspond to the natural business cycle rather than to the calendar year.

fixed-income funds
Mutual funds that purchase bonds to generate interest income or stocks to yield higher-than-average dividends.

forward P/E
A variation of the P/E ratio in which estimated earnings for the coming year are used in place of the latest reported actual earnings.

front-end sales load
An alternative name for the load, so called because a sales commission is deducted from an investment before funds are used to buy mutual fund shares.

fundamental analysis
The study of financial statements and the trends revealed in the numbers, to identify a company's revenue and earnings history and capital strength. The purpose is to identify companies representing the best investment value.

fundamental risk
The risk that financial reports on which investors rely may not be accurate and might even mislead investors in extreme cases.

gapping behavior
Differences in price levels between one day's closing price and the next day's opening price, especially when this incidence is repetitive or frequent.

gaps
Spaces in trading found between one session's close and the next session's open.

global fund
A type of mutual fund investing in companies outside of the United States or based in the United States but serving an international market.

gravestone doji
A bearish doji with an upper shadow only, which looks like a capital T turned upside down.

greed and panic risk
The risk that buying will occur irrationally when prices are running up too far and too fast, or that selling will occur when prices are falling rapidly.

gross profit
The dollar value remaining when the cost of goods sold, or direct costs, is subtracted from revenue.

growth stocks
Stocks of companies expected to report better-than-average earnings and to experience rapid stock price growth as a result, at least for the period in which the growth industry remains in an uptrend.

guidance
Information provided by a company forecasting future revenues and profits, to be used by analysts and investors to judge price performance.

hammer
A candle with a small real body of either color, and a long lower shadow. It appears at the bottom of a downtrend and, if confirmed, indicates a bullish reversal.

hanging man
A candle with a small real body of either color, and a long lower shadow. It appears at the top of an uptrend and, if confirmed, indicates a bearish reversal.

harami
A two-candlestick pattern with a set-up day containing a higher high and a lower low. A bull harami consists of a black set-up followed by a white day, and a bear harami has a white set-up day followed by a black second day.

head and shoulders
A pattern in chart analysis consisting of three price spikes. The first and third (shoulders) are lower than the second (head). After the failed attempt at driving prices upward, price is expected to react by trending downward after the head and shoulders.

hedge funds
Companies usually set up as private partnerships and with a limited number of high–net worth investors, specializing in high-return, high-risk leveraged market positions.

horizontal spreads
Spreads opened with options on the same underlying stock with identical strike prices but different expiration months.

implied volatility
The level of volatility and risk in options trading, comparing current prices of options to established pricing models. The greater the gap between current market value and the pricing model price level, the higher the market volatility.

in the money
The status of an option when current value is higher than the call's strike or lower than the put's strike.

income statement
A financial statement summarizing revenue, costs, earnings, and profits for a specified period of time, usually a quarter or fiscal year.

index funds
Mutual funds that invest in market-tracking indexes rather than directly in equity or debt positions.

inflation risk
The risk of losing purchasing power in money as a consequence of rising prices over time; for investors, inflation requires ever-higher returns on investment to offset the effects of inflation.

insider trading
The act of trading in the market based on information not available to the general public and provided by a source inside an organization or in a position to know news the general public does not have.

institutional investors
Shareholders in publicly listed companies representing the majority of shares held, including mutual funds, pension programs, and insurance companies, as well as other concerns managing the investments of others.

intangible assets
Assets lacking physical value, including goodwill and covenants not to compete.

intra-day trading
A variation of day trading, a strategy in which positions are opened and closed within single trading sessions or, at the most, two consecutive sessions.

intrinsic value
The portion of an option's premium when the current value of stock is higher than the call's strike or lower than the put's strike.

investment club
A group of individuals who pool their money together and share research to select stocks for purchase over a period of time.

investment strategy
A set of rules and procedures an investor develops for picking the elements of a portfolio, identifying desired rates of return and risk levels, and determining when to sell.

investor
An individual most likely to select companies based on fundamental strength and to buy stock with the intention of holding it over many months or years.

Japanese candlesticks
Alternative name for candlesticks and for the charts on which they are used.

knowledge and experience risk
The combined information you have gathered through research and observation, plus past investing and related activities; together, knowledge and experience ultimately determines how you view the markets and how you approach selection of stocks.

large-cap
A classification of companies whose total equity value is greater than $10 billion.

last trading day
The final trading day for options, which is the trading day immediately before the third Saturday of the expiration month.

leverage risk
The risk resulting from borrowing money to invest. In the case of losses, leveraged positions not only have to be paid back, but losses have to be made up as well.

line chart
A simplified chart for tracking a stock's price, consisting of a single line connected between days, and normally reflecting the stock's closing price for each session.

liquidity risk
In the public exchanges, the possibility that high volume will curtail the availability of cash needed to complete trades in shares of stock.

listed company
A corporation whose shares are listed, quoted, and traded over a public exchange, with shares held publicly by either institutional or retail investors.

load funds
Mutual funds that deduct a sales commission from all investments made, to be paid to a salesperson who recommends the investment.

long candle
A candle with an unusually long real body, either white or black, and likely to foreshadow reversal when it appears at the end of a trend.

long position
Ownership of shares, accomplished by a buy order and involving the sequence buy-hold-sell.

long-legged doji
A doji with exceptionally long upper and lower shadows, with the small real body about halfway in the formation. This may be bullish or bearish depending on where it appears in the trend.

long-term assets
The net value (basis minus accumulated depreciation) of capital assets, including real estate, autos and trucks, machinery and equipment, furniture and furnishings, and tools.

long-term liabilities
All debts of a company owed beyond the next 12 months, including notes, contracts, and bonds.

lost opportunity risk
The risk that capital will be fully committed so that new investment opportunities cannot be taken, reducing future profits.

lower shadow
The vertical portion of a candlestick extending below the real body and representing a failed attempt during the session to move the price lower.

MACD
A popular technical indicator, meaning moving average convergence/divergence, the study of trends based on the proximity between price and averages.

management fee
The fee charged by a mutual fund to compensate its professional managers.

margin account
An account provided to investors by their brokers, allowing them to borrow up to one-half of the value of their portfolio.

margin call
A requirement that investors deposit additional funds to meet minimum margin requirements. If the margin call cannot be met, the broker will sell some or all of the portfolio assets.

market capitalization
The total dollar value of a company's net worth, including the most frequently used classifications of large-cap, mid-cap, and small-cap.

market risk
The risk that prices will decline, reducing the value of stocks, potentially for many months; market risk is the best-known and best-understood form of risk.

marubozu
A long candle, white or black, with no shadows or a shadow only above or only below the real body.

mega-cap
Companies with equity value above $200 billion.

micro-cap
Companies with equity value between $50 million and $300 million.

mid-cap
A classification of companies whose total equity value is between $2 and $10 billion.

minor trend
A price trend of only a few days, moving either upward or downward.

momentum oscillators
Indicators that measure the strength or weakness in price as well as the speed of changes. These include tests of moving averages or the Relative Strength Index (RSI).

momentum trading
A system of day trading based solely on identifying short-term trends and timing entry and exit based on the trend's strength or weakness (momentum).

money market funds
Mutual funds that buy only short-term money market instruments, and provide income but no growth to investors.

mortgage pool
A type of pooled investment in which shares consist of part ownership in a pool of secured mortgage contracts.

moving average (MA)
The average price over a fixed number of sessions, adjusted for each new session by removing the oldest and replacing it with the newest day, and then dividing the total by the total number of days.

mutual fund
An investment company designed to combine the capital of many individuals to create a single portfolio designed to meet specified investment and risk objectives.

naked call
Alternative name for an uncovered call.

narrow range day (NRD)
A trading session in which opening and closing prices are very close or identical, indicating exhaustion of the trend and a likely reversal about to occur.

net asset value (NAV)
The day's ending value of a mutual fund, computed by adding the total asset value of the fund (minus any liabilities) and dividing the net total by the number of shares outstanding.

net operating profit
The dollar value remaining when all expenses are deducted from gross profit.

net profit
The bottom line, the final profit when all adjustments and deductions have been made.

net worth
The dollar value of a company's equity value (assets less liabilities), divided into capital stock and retained earnings (the sum of all profits and losses from year to year) and other equity adjustments.

no-load funds
Mutual funds that are purchased without deduction of a sales load, or commission.

OHLC chart
A stock chart showing each session's trading range by way of a vertical stick, as well as opening and closing price noted by small horizontal sticks.

open-end fund
A type of mutual fund that does not place limits on its number of subscribers or assets it manages.

opening order
An order placed with a broker to create a position, either long or short.

options
Intangible contracts allowing their holders to control 100 shares of a specific stock for a fraction of the cost of trading those shares.

oscillators
Technical indicators that track price movement and identify overbought or oversold conditions. These aid in picking the best entry and exit points in trades.

out of the money
The status of an option when current value is lower than the call's strike or higher than the put's strike.

overdiversification
Condition when a portfolio is spread so broadly that exceptional advantages in some holdings are offset by underperformance in others, resulting in a poor overall return.

paper trading
A system of simulated investing in which a portfolio of cash can be used to buy shares of stock based on actual value in the current stock market. However, because it is a simulation, there is no risk. The purpose to paper trading is to demonstrate to a new investor how the markets work.

pattern day trader
Any trader who moves in and out of positions in the same stock four or more times within five consecutive trading sessions and who is required to maintain at least $25,000 in cash and securities in their brokerage account.

percentage swing
Price movement of a specified percentage below the high or above the low, used to generate entry or exit decisions as part of a swing trading strategy.

political and economic risk
The risk that outside influences may affect stock valuation. Political changes, either domestic or international, may curtail activities or affect customers; economic activities may slow down production, prevent expansion, or prevent companies from hiring or retaining employees.

preferred stock
Classification of ownership with priority in dividend payments and liquidation above both debtors and common stockholders; however, preferred stockholders have no voting rights.

premium
The value of an option. This is expressed as a numeral without a dollar sign and with two decimal places, denoting the value per share. A premium of 2.40, for example, means the option is priced at $240.

prepaid assets
Expenses paid in one year but properly assigned to two or more years, set up as an asset to be amortized properly to future periods.

pretax profit
The net profit earned for a quarter or a fiscal year, before calculating the liability for income taxes; the net left when other income and expenses are added to or subtracted from net operating profit.

price/earnings ratio (P/E)
A comparison between the current price per share and the latest reported earnings per share, indicating the current market perception of future earnings potential.

price-weighted average
A kind of stock market average in which the prices of components are added together and divided by the number of stocks used; the result is that higher-priced stocks have more influence on the average than lower-priced stocks.

primary trend
The overall direction of the market, either bullish or bearish, that lasts from a few months to several years.

prospectus
A disclosure document explaining the nature and risks of securities, including management and their compensation, investment objectives, and costs involved in buying shares.

public participation phase
The second phase of a trend, in which the market follows the lead of those in the accumulation phase and buys or sells shares in the indicated direction.

pump and dump
The purchase of shares and encouragement of others to do the same, hoping to drive prices higher and then sell at a profit.

purchasing power
The value of money when compared between years. As inflation rises, the dollar loses its purchasing power compared to past years.

put
An option providing its owner the right but not the obligation to sell 100 shares of a specified stock, at a fixed price, on or before a specified expiration date.

random walk theory
A theory stating that stock prices cannot be predicted using any fundamental or technical indicators, because price behavior is entirely random and unpredictable.

range flip
The observed change after a price breakout, in which previous resistance becomes new support in an uptrend, or in which previous support becomes new resistance in a downtrend.

real body
The middle rectangle of a candlestick, showing whether the session moved upward (white) or downward (black), and making it possible to spot trends immediately.

real estate investment trust (REIT)
A real estate investment conduit that trades on public exchanges like shares of stock.

real estate mortgage investment conduit (REMIC)
A mortgage pool offered by a government-sponsored or government-guaranteed mortgage organization.

record date
The date on which recorded owners of stock earn a declared dividend even though payment does not take place until several weeks after; normally two trading days after the ex-dividend date.

redemption fee
A charge assessed by a mutual fund at the time shares are redeemed, not to exceed 2 percent of the redemption value.

reinvested dividends
Those dividends used to automatically purchase additional shares of stock as opposed to taking payments in cash. Reinvested dividends earn the dividend yield at a compounded rate because future dividend payments are based on the total shares held, including shares purchased with quarterly dividends.

Relative Strength Index (RSI)
An oscillator that tracks upward and downward sessions and compares them to quantify momentum and provide an estimate of overbought or oversold conditions.

resistance
The highest price in a stock's trading range, or the high side of the price range at which both sides can agree to a trade.

resistance zone
A range of prices representing resistance, used in place of a single price.

retail investors
Individuals who own shares in publicly traded companies through direct ownership (as opposed to buying shares in mutual funds).

retained earnings
The accumulated sum of a corporation's after-tax net profits, increased each year a profit is reported, and reduced whenever a net loss occurs.

return on assets (ROA)
A ratio comparing net return for a fiscal year, to total assets as of the end of that year. The purpose behind ROA is to calculate the effective investment in assets for the generation of profits.

return on equity (ROE)
A ratio comparing net return from operations to the value of shareholders' equity, used to measure the effective use of invested capital to generate profits.

return on invested capital (ROIC)
A ratio comparing net return adjusted for dividends paid, to total capital. This demonstrates how effectively a company uses its available resources to generate profits.

reversal day
The end of a trend; a session that moves in the direction opposite the established direction, signaling a high possibility of a reversal in the price direction.

reverse head and shoulders
A chart pattern involving three bottom price spikes. The first and third (reverse shoulders) are not as low as the second (the head). After the failed downward movement, prices are expected to reverse and trend upward.

risk
Exposure to loss resulting from numerous market, economic, and company-specific causes.

risk tolerance
The degree of risk appropriate to each individual based on experience and knowledge, available capital, income, and willingness or unwillingness to take chances.

rolling strategy
Closing a short option and replacing it with another option that expires later, with the intention of deferring or avoiding exercise.

round-trip trade
The complete steps involved with first opening and then closing a position.

runaway gap
A pattern of gapping action involving several sessions in close proximity, as part of a trend moving strongly in one direction without offsetting price movement.

sales load
A commission deducted from investments in mutual funds and paid to the salesperson.

secondary market
The government-sponsored market for purchasing of mortgage contracts from lenders, organizing them into larger mortgage pools and selling shares to investors.

secondary trend
A trend lasting from a few days to a few months, with prices moving counter to the direction of the primary trend.

sector risk
A risk identified with a particular sector and its industries, derived from business cycles, market conditions, or economic changes.

sell to close/buy to close
The type of closing order being placed. A sell to close is used to close an existing long position, and a buy to close is used to close an existing short position.

set-up signals
Patterns or changes in price or volume that tell day traders and swing traders when likely trend reversals are about to take place.

shadows
The portion of a candlestick above or below the real body, representing the extent of trading range beyond opening and closing prices.

shareholder service fees
A mutual fund's charge for expenses of responding to client inquiries, either as part of a 12b-1 fee or separately from it.

shares
Part ownership of a corporation that is listed publicly. Shares are bought and sold over public exchanges. Owners of shares are entitled to receive dividends and common stock owners are allowed to vote on matters of corporate management. Shares of stock rise and fall in value every day based on the ever-changing levels of supply and demand.

short covering
Buying activity resulting from holders of shorted stock closing positions; when short covering occurs at a high volume, it may create an artificially high buy indicator.

short position
The sale of shares, accomplished with an opening sell order and involving the sequence sell-hold-buy.

short position risk
The risk incurred by selling as an opening step, in which traders hope for a price decline so the short position can be closed (bought), and the net difference will be a profit.

short selling
The act of borrowing stock and then selling it in the hope that the price will fall. If that occurs, shares can be closed by buying at a lower price. If the stock price rises, it creates a loss because the short position has to be closed (bought) at a higher price. Short sellers also have to pay interest on the shares borrowed to open the short position.

simple interest
Interest calculated at its annual rate and without compounding; for example, dividend yield represents the simple interest paid on stock each year.

small-cap
A classification of companies whose total equity value is less than $2 billion.

specialty funds
Mutual funds that select portfolios based on a specific theme such as social consciousness.

speculation
Short-term trading based on price movement in order to maximize profits based on immediate price movements and trends, distinguished from investment, which tends to involve longer-term hold periods.

spinning top
A candle with a small real body and long upper and lower shadows of about the same size; the spinning top is either bullish or bearish depending on where it is found.

spreads
Option strategies combining two or more options on the same underlying stock, but with different strikes, or different expiration dates, or both.

squeeze alert
A series of three consecutive candle sessions. A bull squeeze alert consists of black candles, and a bear squeeze alert has three white candles. In both cases, each day's high is lower than the previous, and each day's low is higher than the previous.

straddles
Option strategies involving opening of call and put positions with the same strike and expiration.

strike
The fixed price of an option, at which the owner is allowed to trade 100 shares of stock.

supply and demand
The economic forces that set prices for publicly traded stocks. When buyers want more shares than are immediately available from sellers, the excess demand drives up prices. When sellers want to sell more shares than buyers want to buy, the excess supply forces prices down. The interactive supply-and-demand forces are continuous.

support
The lowest price in a stock's trading range, or the low side of the price range at which sellers and buyers are able to agree on price.

support zone
A range of prices representing support, used in place of a single price.

swing trading
A short-term trading strategy based on recognition of trends lasting only a few days (usually three to five), with entry and exit based on set-up signals.

synthetic position
An option position involving two or more open contracts designed to act in the same manner as another security, such as stock.

tails
Alternative name for a candlestick's shadows, especially when longer than average.

tangible book value
The net capital value of a company (assets minus liabilities) further reduced for all intangible assets. When the tangible value is divided by outstanding shares of stock, the result is the tangible book value per share.

tax risk
The risk that after-tax return on investment will fall short of the return needed to preserve spending power after inflation.

tax-free bond funds
Mutual funds that invest solely in municipal bonds that offer tax-free interest to investors.

technical analysis
The study of price patterns, charts, and trends to time entry and exit into positions in stock, compared to fundamental analysis, which studies trends to pick companies.

technical knowledge and experience risk
The risk that a range of technical indicators is difficult to explain without a background in interpreting them and recognizing their significance and effect on price trends.

technical risk
Any risk directly involving price, reflected in price volatility and trends as well as in related indicators such as trading volume.

terms
The four attributes of every option that cannot be changed or replaced: type of option (call or put), strike, expiration date, and underlying security.

three black crows
A bearish candlestick formation of three consecutive sessions. All three are black. Each day's closing price is lower than the preceding close and each day's opening price is lower than the previous day's open.

three white soldiers
A bullish candlestick formation of three consecutive sessions. All three are white. Each day's closing price is higher than the preceding close and each day's opening price is higher than the previous day's open.

time value
The portion of an option's premium that varies with time remaining to expiration; the further away expiration date, the higher the time value. This value declines gradually until the last two months, when time value falls rapidly, ending at zero on expiration day.

total capitalization
The combination of long-term debt (debt capitalization) and net worth (equity capitalization).

trader
An individual who buys and sells stock based on short-term price trends, who is focused on stock price changes rather than on the financial history of the company.

trading halt
The temporary suspension of trading in a particular security in anticipation of an imbalance that may be created by upcoming announcements of mergers or acquisitions, or negotiations between companies.

trading range
The distance between recent high and low price levels; the price area in which buyers and sellers currently interact with one another.

trend
The established direction or movement of price, or changes in an indicator, that define a company's value over many months or years.

trend line
A straight line drawn beneath a rising support level or above a falling resistance level. Once price levels reverse and interrupt the line, a reversal may be indicated or confirmed.

triangle
A trend involving changes in the breadth of the trading range. As the range narrows during the current trend direction, the likelihood of reversal increases.

true range
A recalculated trading range including not only a single session, but the range between one session's closing price and the next session's high.

uncovered call
A short call written when the trader does not also own 100 shares of the underlying stock; a high-risk option strategy.

underdiversification
A common condition in which a portfolio is focused on too few stocks or on stocks exposed to the same market risks.

underlying security
The stock or other security controlled by the option. In the case of options on stock, every option contract controls 100 shares of the underlying security.

unit investment trust (UIT)
A fund that purchases income-generating securities (bonds and stocks) and creates a trust in which shares are sold to investors. Periodic payments are made for interest, dividends, and capital gains earned throughout the life of the UIT.

upper shadow
The vertical portion of a candlestick extending above the real body and representing a failed attempt during the session to move the price higher.

uptrend
In swing trading, a series of consecutive sessions with higher high prices and higher low prices in each session, compared to the previous session.

value investing
A method for picking long-term investments by determining their true value and quality, and then seeking discounted prices to find bargains.

variable annuity
A product similar to a mutual fund, which combines investment dollars from many individuals to create a portfolio. The issuing company agrees to make a series of payments in future years based on the value of contributed capital and performance of the securities in the portfolio.

vertical spreads
Spreads opened with options on the same underlying stock with identical expiration dates but different strike prices.

volatility
The degree of price change within a defined period of time, used as a measurement of market risk in a particular stock.

volatility risk
A technical variation on the broader market risk, involving the degree of exposure traders accept in picking and timing positions in stock.

volume
The level of trading in a stock, represented by the number of shares exchanged between buyers and sellers in a specified period of time (a trading day, for example).

volume spike
A single trading session with higher-than-average volume, signaling the possibility of a coming reversal of price movement.

wedge
A price pattern in which the trading range narrows time, often representing a disruption in an uptrend before that trend resumes.

Western technical indicators
The traditional technical patterns and developments used in technical analysis to time entry and exit from trading positions.

wicks
Alternative name for a candlestick's shadows.

working capital
The cash available to the organization to pay current obligations and to fund future growth and pay dividends; a fundamental test of money management.

writer
A trader who opens, or writes, a short position in options.

RECOMMENDED READING

Arnold, Glen. 2009. *Value Investing*. Upper Saddle River, NJ: Financial
Times/Prentice Hall.

Brady, James. 2012. *Income Investing*. New York: McGraw-Hill.

Brooks, Al. 2011. *Trading Price Action Trends*. Hoboken, NJ: John Wiley
& Sons.

Dorsey, Pat. 2004. *The Five Rules for Successful Stock Investing*.
Hoboken, NJ: John Wiley & Sons.

Fontanills, George A., and Gentile, Tom. 2001. *The Stock Market
Course*. Hoboken, NJ: John Wiley & Sons.

Greenblatt, Joel. 2011. *The Big Secret for the Small Investor*.
New York: Crown Business.

O'Neil, William. 2009. *How to Make Money in Stocks,* 4th Ed.
New York, NY: McGraw-Hill.

Sincere, Michael. 2003. *Understanding Stocks*. New York: McGraw-Hill.

Thomsett, Michael C. 2006. *Getting Started in Fundamental Analysis*.
Hoboken, NJ: John Wiley & Sons.

Tilson, Whitney and Tongue, Glenn. 2012. *The Art of Value Investing*.
Hoboken, NJ: John Wiley & Sons.

ABOUT THE AUTHOR

MICHAEL C. THOMSETT (www.MichaelThomsett.com) has written more than 70 books on investing, real estate, business, and management. He is author of several Wiley books, including the eight editions of the bestselling *Getting Started in Options*, as well as *Getting Started in Fundamental Analysis*, *Getting Started in Real Estate Investing*, and *Getting Started in Swing Trading*. He also has written numerous other stock investing and trading books, including *Winning with Stocks* (Amacom Books), *Stock Profits* (FT Press), and *Mastering Fundamental Analysis* and *Mastering Technical Analysis* (Dearborn Press). The author contributes regularly to many websites, including the CBOE, Benzinga, Seeking Alpha and on his website, ThomsettOptions.com; and writes articles for the *AAII Journal* and NAIC's *Better Investing*. He also teaches five classes at the New York Institute of Finance (NYIF). Thomsett has been writing professionally since 1978 and full time since 1985. He lives near Nashville, Tennessee.

INDEX